MAYER SMITH

A Curse Between Heartbeats

Copyright © 2025 by Mayer Smith

All rights reserved. No part of this publication may be reproduced, stored or transmitted in any form or by any means, electronic, mechanical, photocopying, recording, scanning, or otherwise without written permission from the publisher. It is illegal to copy this book, post it to a website, or distribute it by any other means without permission.

This novel is entirely a work of fiction. The names, characters and incidents portrayed in it are the work of the author's imagination. Any resemblance to actual persons, living or dead, events or localities is entirely coincidental.

Mayer Smith asserts the moral right to be identified as the author of this work.

Mayer Smith has no responsibility for the persistence or accuracy of URLs for external or third-party Internet Websites referred to in this publication and does not guarantee that any content on such Websites is, or will remain, accurate or appropriate.

Designations used by companies to distinguish their products are often claimed as trademarks. All brand names and product names used in this book and on its cover are trade names, service marks, trademarks and registered trademarks of their respective owners. The publishers and the book are not associated with any product or vendor mentioned in this book. None of the companies referenced within the book have endorsed the book.

First edition

*This book was professionally typeset on Reedsy.
Find out more at reedsy.com*

Contents

1	The Heartbeat That Isn't Mine	1
2	The Prince in the Mirror	8
3	A Fae's Dying Wish	16
4	The Curse Awakens	25
5	A Heartbeat Away From Death	34
6	The Fae and the Mortal Girl	43
7	The Queen's Forbidden Spell	51
8	The Shadows That Watch	59
9	A Prince on the Edge of Oblivion	67
10	A Heart Split in Two	76
11	A Name I Once Knew	85
12	The Other Half of the Curse	95
13	The Court of the Unseen	104
14	The Betrayal in His Eyes	114
15	Love Is Not a Chain	124
16	The Fade Begins	134
17	A Love That Never Belonged to Me	145
18	The Final Beat	154
19	A Curse Undone, A Soul Unraveled	162
20	A Soul Unraveled	172

One

The Heartbeat That Isn't Mine

Elara had learned to live with it.

The second heartbeat. The one that pulsed just beneath her own, always present, always faint. Sometimes, it followed the rhythm of her own heart, beating in tandem like a whispered echo, soft and subtle enough that she could pretend it wasn't there. Other times, it stuttered—faltering when her emotions swayed, racing when her pulse did not, slowing when fear clenched her ribs.

She had spent years convincing herself that it was nothing. That it was a strange quirk of her body. That she was imagining it.

But deep down, Elara knew better.

A Curse Between Heartbeats

She felt it most in the stillness of the night when the world was quiet, and her heartbeat drummed steadily beneath her ribs. That was when the other pulse betrayed itself—throbbing softly as if it belonged to someone else. Someone near. Someone unseen.

Tonight was one of those nights.

Elara lay in bed, her eyes locked on the ceiling, her fingers resting lightly against her collarbone. She could feel her own heart there, steady and strong. And beneath it, the faint tremor of another.

It was fading.

Her throat tightened. This had happened before, though not often. The second heartbeat had always been constant, inescapable, but sometimes, it would grow weaker as if it was struggling. As if it was dying.

And when it did, an ache formed in her chest, raw and unexplainable.

Elara turned her head toward the window. The night outside was dark, the town's distant streetlights casting long shadows along the walls of her room. The old house groaned as the wind swept through the trees outside, a whispery sound that sent a shiver down her spine.

She should have been used to it.

The Heartbeat That Isn't Mine

I should have been used to all of it.

But tonight, something felt different. The air was too still. The shadows stretched too long. And the heartbeat—the heartbeat wasn't just fading anymore.

It was struggling.

Elara sat up abruptly, her pulse spiking. The moment she moved, the second heartbeat reacted—fluttering and faltering like a bird caught in a storm.

She pressed a hand to her chest, willing it to steady.

Why? Why did it feel so much weaker than before?

She had tried to tell people once.

Her mother dismissed it, claiming it was just in her head. Her doctor laughed and said it was probably nothing—an overactive imagination, a trick of the nerves.

But Elara knew the truth. She had known it since she was a child.

This heartbeat did not belong to her.

And tonight, for the first time in her life, she was afraid it might disappear completely.

She slid out of bed, her bare feet hitting the cold floor. The room suddenly felt more minor, the walls pressing in, and the weight of the silence made it harder to breathe.

She didn't know why, but instinct told her to move, to do something, to stop whatever was happening.

But how?

Her fingers curled into the fabric of her nightshirt, her thoughts racing. What would happen if the heartbeat vanished? Would she feel different? Would she—

A flicker of movement in the mirror stopped her breath.

Elara froze.

The mirror stood against the far wall, just beside her closet. It was old, the edges worn with time, the surface speckled with imperfections. The reflection showed only her room, the dim glow of the moonlight casting everything in muted silver.

But for a second—just for a second—she swore she had seen something.

A figure.

Golden eyes.

She sucked in a breath, her body locking into place. Her heart pounded, and beneath it, the second heartbeat thudded harder.

The Heartbeat That Isn't Mine

It was reacting.

To what?

She took a cautious step forward. Her reflection moved with her, unchanged. She scanned the corners of the glass, her pulse ringing in her ears. There was nothing there now. Nothing at all.

A trick of the light. It had to be.

But then, why did the second heartbeat feel stronger?

"Elara."

The whisper came from nowhere.

She spun around, her breath catching, but the room was empty. The shadows hadn't moved, the door remained shut, and the only sound was the distant rustling of trees beyond her window.

Yet someone had spoken.

Someone had said her name.

Her skin prickled with a deep, unsettling fear.

"Elara," the voice whispered again.

This time, it came from the mirror.

A Curse Between Heartbeats

Her stomach dropped.

The air in the room seemed too thin, the space between her and the glass stretching and contracting like a living thing. A pulse throbbed at her temples, and the second heartbeat was no longer weak. It was no longer fading.

It was racing.

As if something had woken it up.

Elara took a slow, deliberate step toward the mirror, her breath shallow. The reflection of her room wavered, the darkness shifting at the edges, curling like smoke.

Then, just as she reached out—

The glass shuddered.

She gasped, stumbling back. The surface rippled as if touched by water, distorting her reflection. And then—

A hand.

A pale, elegant hand pressed against the inside of the glass, fingers splayed.

Her stomach twisted, her throat closing around a scream.

And behind the hand, half-hidden in shadow, golden eyes stared back at her.

The Heartbeat That Isn't Mine

The second heartbeat thundered in her chest.

"Elara," the stranger murmured.

And then, before she could move, before she could even think—

The mirror shattered.

A gust of icy air exploded through the room, knocking her backwards. She hit the floor hard, pain shooting through her palms as shards of glass scattered around her. The wind howled through the space like a living thing, rushing from the mirror's broken remains.

She tried to breathe, to move, but her body was frozen in terror.

And then, through the chaos, through the swirling air and the dying echoes of breaking glass—

She heard it.

The second heartbeat.

Loud. Clear.

And no longer inside her.

It was standing right in front of her.

Two

The Prince in the Mirror

E lara could not move.

The room felt colder, as if something had drained all its warmth, leaving only a hollow, aching silence. Shards of the shattered mirror lay scattered around her, reflecting fractured moonlight pieces. A wind that should not have been there still swirled in the air, rattling against her skin like invisible hands.

And then there was him.

The figure who had stepped from the broken glass.

He stood just beyond the wreckage, half-shrouded in shadows. His golden eyes glowed softly in the dim light, their brilliance stark against the darkness curling around him. His features were sharp, unnaturally perfect—high cheekbones, a strong jawline, and lips pressed into a thin, unreadable line.

But it wasn't his beauty that made Elara's breath catch.

It was the way he was looking at her.

Like he had known her forever.

Like he had been waiting for this moment.

Her body screamed at her to run, to bolt for the door, to put as much distance between herself and this stranger as possible. But she couldn't. She was frozen in place, her heartbeat slamming against her ribs in wild, erratic beats.

Or was it hers?

Because there was another rhythm beneath it, one that matched the presence standing before her. A heartbeat—his heartbeat.

The heartbeat that had never belonged to her.

A sudden rush of dizziness washed over her, and she barely managed to push herself up onto shaking arms. The stranger didn't move, didn't speak, only watched her with an intensity that made her feel stripped bare.

Elara swallowed hard, forcing her voice to work. "Who—who are you?"

A flicker of something passed across his face. Something unreadable. Then, finally, he spoke.

"You know me," he said.

His voice was low, edged with something ancient, something that made the hair on the back of her neck rise.

Elara shook her head. "No. I don't."

The corner of his lips twitched, not quite a smile. "You do."

Anger, fueled by the fear still gripping her, flared in her chest. "Don't play games with me. I don't know who you are."

His expression darkened. "You don't remember."

"Remember what?"

Instead of answering, he took a step toward her.

Elara scrambled back, her hands grazing over sharp glass. She winced but didn't dare take her eyes off him.

He stopped. His gaze flicked to her hands, then back to her face. "You're hurt."

His voice had softened, but Elara didn't trust it.

She forced herself to her feet, legs trembling beneath her. She refused to cower. "Stay back," she warned.

The Prince in the Mirror

His head tilted slightly, like he was studying her reaction. "You fear me."

"Of course I do! You—" she motioned wildly to the broken mirror, to him, to everything. "You just stepped out of my mirror. Like it was a door. Normal people don't do that."

A faint shadow of amusement crossed his face. "I'm not normal."

Elara's breath hitched. She knew that. She had known it the second she saw him. No human had eyes like that. No human had a presence that made the air itself feel alive.

Her voice dropped to a whisper. "What are you?"

Silence stretched between them.

Then, finally, he said, "Fae."

The word sent a cold shiver down her spine.

Elara had heard the old stories. The warnings. The myths whispered in bedtime tales—about fae who stole names, who lured mortals into their world, who wove curses with words laced in silver lies.

They weren't real.

They couldn't be real.

A Curse Between Heartbeats

And yet—one was standing right in front of her.

Elara gripped the edge of her nightshirt, forcing herself to stay calm. "What do you want?"

For the first time, hesitation flickered across his face. Then, softer, "You."

A chill swept through her veins. "What?"

His golden eyes searched hers, and for a moment, something in his expression almost looked... pained.

Then he said the words that shattered her world.

"My heartbeat is inside you, Elara."

A sharp intake of breath filled her lungs.

No. No, that wasn't possible.

He took another step forward. "You've felt it, haven't you? The second heartbeat. The one that does not belong to you."

Elara shook her head, backing away. "That doesn't mean anything."

"It means everything." His voice was quiet, heavy with something she couldn't name. "It means you are the only thing tethering me to this world."

Her mind spun, trying to grasp the meaning of his words. "What are you talking about?"

His gaze didn't waver. "If you stop loving me—I will fade from existence."

A stunned silence filled the room.

Elara's pulse pounded, her skin ice-cold. "I—I don't even know you."

The corner of his mouth twitched, but there was no amusement in it. "You did once."

A sharp pain stabbed behind her eyes—fleeting, but strong enough to make her wince.

Flashes of something—of somewhere—rushed through her mind. A silver lake beneath a sky filled with strange, glowing stars. A whispered name. Fingers brushing against her skin, warmth blooming beneath the touch.

The moment was gone before she could hold onto it.

Her breath came fast, uneven. "No. I don't—I don't remember."

"I know." There was something raw in his voice. "That is part of the curse."

Curse.

A Curse Between Heartbeats

The word struck her like a physical blow.

Elara's fingers curled into her palms. "What curse?"

His jaw tightened. "The one that binds us."

The one that stole his heartbeat and placed it inside her. The one that tied their existences together, whether she wanted it or not.

And worst of all—the one that meant she held his life in her hands.

Elara took a shuddering breath, her chest tightening with too many emotions at once. Fear. Confusion. A strange, terrible ache she couldn't explain.

The fae prince—because that's what he had to be—watched her, his golden eyes heavy with expectation.

She wanted to run. Wanted to pretend this was a nightmare she could wake from.

But deep down, beneath the panic, beneath the doubt—

She knew.

She had always known.

The heartbeat inside her had never been her own.

And now, standing in front of her, was the man it belonged to.

Three

A Fae's Dying Wish

The room still smelled like shattered glass and something ancient—like the damp air before a storm, laced with the faint scent of something floral and strange. The fae prince stood before Elara, his golden eyes watching her, and his weight pressed against her chest, stealing her breath.

She had not moved from where she stood, her body tense, heart pounding against her ribs like a warning drum.

Or was it his heart?

The thought sent another wave of cold through her, settling deep in her bones.

"Elara," he said softly, as if speaking her name alone carried the weight of an entire world.

She flinched, stepping back, her bare foot brushing against a shard of glass. She sucked in a sharp breath as the sting lanced through her skin, but she didn't let her gaze waver.

The prince frowned, shifting slightly. "You're bleeding."

"Don't," she snapped, pressing her back against the nearest wall. "Don't act like you care."

He exhaled, slow and steady. "I do care."

Her throat clenched. "How can you care about someone you don't even know?"

His eyes darkened, something flickering beneath their golden depths. "That's not true."

Elara clenched her fists. "Then tell me the truth."

For a moment, he said nothing.

Then he moved. Not forward, not back—just a slight shift of his shoulders, the motion like a caged animal testing its boundaries.

"I don't have much time." His voice was quiet, but it carried a weight that made her stomach clench.

She didn't know why, but those words made something shift

in her chest. "Time for what?"

He hesitated.

Then, carefully, he said, "To live."

The world tilted.

Elara pressed herself harder against the wall, shaking her head. "No. No, you don't get to come out of my mirror, tell me my heartbeat isn't mine, and then—then say you're dying."

Something like sorrow flickered across his face, gone before she could grasp it. "I am already fading."

The words sent an unexpected pang through her. She didn't understand why. She didn't know him. She shouldn't care.

And yet—

She could feel it.

The way the second heartbeat had weakened over the years. The way it sometimes slowed when she felt empty, when she let herself sink into loneliness.

Her breath hitched. "Because of me?"

His expression was unreadable. "Because of the curse."

Elara swallowed, the air in the room pressing down on her.

"What curse?"

The prince's gaze dropped slightly, as if he were weighing his words. Then, at last, he spoke.

"A long time ago," he said, voice barely above a whisper, "a fae queen wove a spell that bound my life to another's heart." His eyes met hers again, steady. "To yours."

Elara felt something twist in her chest. "Why?"

His lips pressed together. "Because I was never meant to survive."

The words struck like a blade against stone.

A strange, eerie silence settled between them. The wind outside rattled against the windowpane, whispering against the broken shards of glass on the floor.

Elara's voice was barely a breath. "What does that mean?"

The fae prince exhaled, slow and measured.

"I was born under a dying star," he murmured. "The queen—my mother—was told I would not live past my twenty-first year." His eyes flickered with something unreadable. "And she would not allow that to happen."

Elara's fingers curled into her palms, knuckles white. "So she—she cursed me?"

"No." His gaze darkened. "She cursed you."

The breath rushed from Elara's lungs.

She shook her head, unable to make sense of it. "That doesn't—how could she—why would she do this to me?"

The fae prince's expression didn't change. "Because you were chosen."

The words sent a ripple of something deep through her.

"Chosen?" she echoed. "For what?"

His golden eyes locked onto hers. "To be the one who keeps me alive."

Elara felt the weight of the words settle over her like a heavy, invisible chain.

She had lived her whole life with a second heartbeat in her chest, never knowing what it meant. Never knowing that it did not belong to her. That it belonged to him.

Her breath shuddered. "And if I stop?"

The prince didn't flinch. "I will fade."

The silence that followed was deafening.

Elara wanted to tell him that this wasn't fair. That this wasn't her burden to bear.

But then a thought cut through the storm of her panic.

She looked up sharply. "What happens to me?"

Something flickered in his gaze.

"Elara—"

"What happens," she demanded, stepping forward, "if you fade? What happens to me?"

The fae prince hesitated.

Then, quietly, he said, "Your heart will shatter."

Elara's stomach dropped.

The room swayed around her, the weight of those words knocking the air from her lungs.

She pressed a hand against her chest, against the rhythm that had always been there. The rhythm that was never truly hers.

If he disappeared—if he died—

Would she die, too?

She didn't realize she was trembling until she saw the way his eyes flicked to her hands, to the way her fingers trembled against her nightshirt.

"Elara," he said softly.

She looked up at him, her breath coming fast. "I didn't ask for this."

"I know." His voice was steady. "Neither did I."

The weight of those words settled deep, curling into her bones.

For the first time, she saw the exhaustion behind his golden eyes. The weariness. The quiet resignation of someone who had been fighting for far too long.

A prince with a heartbeat that did not belong to him.

A girl whose life had never been her own.

Elara exhaled shakily. "You said you don't have much time."

He nodded once. "The curse is growing weaker. The bond is breaking."

She swallowed hard. "Because I don't love you."

His lips parted slightly, as if the words had struck him somewhere deeper than she could see.

She almost felt guilty. Almost.

But how could she love someone she had never met? How could she be expected to carry the weight of someone else's existence?

She lifted her chin. "Is that why you're here?"

He was quiet for a long moment.

Then, finally, he said, "I came to ask for something."

Elara braced herself. "What?"

The prince's golden eyes burned into hers.

"I need you to remember."

A strange pressure built behind her ribs. A deep, aching pull, like something inside her recognized his words—like something inside her had been waiting for them.

The moment stretched, thick with something she could not name.

And then—

A whisper of something pressed against her mind.

A name. A voice. A fleeting memory, gone before she could grasp it.

Elara's breath hitched.

The prince stepped forward. Close enough that she could feel the coolness of his presence, the faint hum of magic that seemed to cling to his skin.

"Elara," he said again, voice barely above a whisper. "You have to remember."

The second heartbeat thudded harder.

A pulse of something ancient, something deep.

And then—

The world around her cracked.

Four

The Curse Awakens

Elara's world cracked—not just in her mind but in the air around her.

An ancient and unseen pressure surged through her chest, catching her breath. The room shifted like something had unravelled within it, pulling at the edges of her reality. The space between her and the fae prince, between the present and something lost, seemed to blur.

She staggered, gripping the doorframe for balance as a sudden, crushing weight pressed against her ribs. The second heartbeat—the one that wasn't hers—was thundering now, erratic and wild. It pounded in her ears, drowning out her thoughts, syncing with something profound and unseen.

The fae prince—Rowan—was watching her. His golden eyes

burned with something she couldn't name, something intense and unrelenting.

"Elara," he said, stepping forward.

She flinched. The movement sent a jolt of pain through her skull like something inside her was trying to crack open.

"No," she gasped, pressing her palms to her temples. "No, I don't—"

Then, the whispers began.

Not from him.

Not from the house.

From inside her own head.

Remember.

A soft voice, threading through her consciousness like a silver thread, pulling at something long buried. It wasn't Rowan's voice. It wasn't even hers.

It was something else.

Something older.

"Elara." Rowan's voice reached her again, but it sounded distant. Like he was speaking from across a vast chasm, one she wasn't sure she could cross.

The whispers grew louder.

You were never meant to forget.

The air in the room thickened, heavy with an energy that crackled against her skin like static before a storm. The walls seemed too close, the space shrinking and stretching all at once.

And then, suddenly—

She was no longer in her bedroom.

The shift was instant.

One breath ago, she had been standing in the dim light of her home, surrounded by broken glass and confusion. The next, she was somewhere else entirely.

A vast sky stretched above her, filled with swirling constellations she had never seen before. The stars here did not shine like those in her world—they pulsed, thrumming with energy, like living things. Beneath her feet, the ground was soft, covered in thick grass that shimmered with an unnatural glow.

The air smelled of something sweet and unfamiliar, laced with magic.

And in the distance, a silver lake stretched toward the horizon, its surface rippling though there was no wind.

Elara knew this place.

Somewhere deep inside, in a part of her mind she had never been able to reach, she recognized it.

But she didn't know why.

"Elara."

She turned at the sound of her name.

Rowan was standing there, just a few feet away. But he was different.

His clothes were not the dark, earth-toned garments he had worn in her room. Instead, he was dressed in deep blue, lined with silver thread that shimmered under the starry sky. His golden eyes were filled with something unreadable, something distant.

And in his hand, he held a small vial.

The glass was delicate, almost fragile-looking, filled with a swirling silver liquid that pulsed softly—like a heartbeat.

Elara's stomach twisted.

She knew what it was before he even spoke.

The Curse Awakens

"My heart," he said softly, holding it up to the light.

Her breath caught.

It was beautiful. And terrible.

She couldn't move, couldn't speak.

Because deep inside her, something was unraveling.

Memories—half-formed and fleeting—pressed against her mind.

A night filled with laughter and whispered promises. Fingers brushing against hers. A vow spoken beneath a sky like this one, under these very stars.

And then—pain.

A spell whispered in a foreign tongue.

A scream—hers? His?

A fading heartbeat.

And then, nothing.

Everything went dark.

Elara gasped as she was ripped back into her body.

The force of it sent her staggering, nearly collapsing against the wall. Her chest ached like something had been ripped from it.

Rowan was standing in front of her, eyes wide, breathing just as hard as she was.

"You saw it," he said.

It wasn't a question.

Elara clenched her fists, her pulse racing. "I don't—I don't understand—"

"The curse is waking up," he said, stepping closer. "The memories are breaking through."

She swallowed hard. "That wasn't—no, that wasn't real. It was a dream, or—or something else."

Rowan's expression darkened. "You know that's not true."

Elara shook her head. "I don't—I don't remember that. I've never been there before."

His jaw tightened. "Yes, you have."

A chill swept through her.

The Curse Awakens

Because a part of her knew he was right.

A part of her knew that silver lake. That sky. That heartbeat in his hand.

Because once, it had belonged to her.

A wave of nausea rolled through her. She pressed a hand to her temple, forcing herself to stay upright. "Why now?" she whispered. "Why is it happening now?"

Rowan's eyes flickered with something dark.

"The curse was never meant to last this long," he said quietly. "The magic is breaking. And when it does—"

He didn't finish.

But Elara understood.

When the magic broke, so would the bond.

And when the bond broke—

Rowan would fade.

Panic tightened her throat. "No." She shook her head, voice trembling. "No, this isn't fair. I never agreed to this."

Rowan exhaled, something like regret flickering in his expression. "Neither did I."

Elara's vision blurred. The weight of it all—the memories, the truth, the curse—pressed against her like an invisible force.

But through the haze of it, she felt something else.

The second heartbeat.

Still there.

Still bound to her.

Still weakening.

"Elara," Rowan said softly, stepping closer. "If you don't stop it—"

"I know," she whispered.

Her mind was a storm.

She should have been running. She should have been screaming. She should have been clawing at the walls of her own reality, demanding to wake up from this nightmare.

But instead—

She met Rowan's gaze.

And deep in the depths of his golden eyes, she saw something that made her chest tighten.

Not desperation. Not pleading.

But hope.

And it terrified her.

Five

A Heartbeat Away From Death

Elara's pulse thundered in her ears, but it wasn't hers.

The second heartbeat—the one tethered to the fae prince standing before her—was erratic, each uneven beat echoing inside her chest like a warning bell. It was too fast. Too weak. Too unnatural.

She pressed a trembling hand against her ribcage, feeling the pulse beneath her skin. Her heartbeat pounded strong, steady, full of life. But beneath it, the other was faltering.

Dying.

She lifted her gaze to Rowan.

His golden eyes bore into her, searching, pleading, but not

with words. His face was paler than before, a faint shimmer of magic flickering along his skin like a candle caught in the wind.

Fading.

Elara's breath came sharp and shallow. "What's happening to you?"

Rowan swayed slightly, his fingers curling as if trying to grasp onto something unseen. "It's—" His voice caught, raw and strained. "The curse. It's accelerating."

Her blood turned to ice.

"Because of me," she whispered.

His expression remained unreadable, but his silence was answer enough.

Because she hadn't accepted it.

Because she had denied the bond.

Because she didn't—

Elara shook her head, her chest tightening painfully. "This isn't fair."

She didn't know him. She had never asked for this.

A Curse Between Heartbeats

How could the universe expect her to hold someone else's life? To love someone she had no memory of to keep him from slipping into oblivion?

Rowan's eyes fluttered shut for a moment, his breath shallow. A fine tremor ran through his limbs. "I can feel it pulling me away."

Elara clenched her fists.

No.

No, she wasn't going to let this happen.

Not like this.

Without thinking, she grabbed his wrist. His skin was cold, unnaturally so. The shimmer of magic beneath his skin flickered again, then pulsed at the contact like an ember trying to reignite.

Rowan's breath hitched, his eyes snapping open to meet hers.

"Elara," he murmured.

A strange warmth spread through her palm when she touched him. It travelled up her arm and through her chest, weaving into the erratic second heartbeat inside her.

It wasn't love.

But it was something.

His form solidified slightly, the fading magic stabilising. The sharp angles of his features became more apparent, and the golden glow of his irises became less dim.

But it wasn't enough.

His heartbeat was still too weak. Still flickering like a candle about to be snuffed out.

Elara's pulse raced. "What do I do?"

Rowan exhaled shakily, his fingers curling weakly over hers. "I don't—" His voice cut off as he staggered, barely catching himself before his legs gave out beneath him.

Elara reacted on instinct. She looped his arm around her shoulder, gripping his waist to steady him. His weight was startling—he felt light, too light as if he were already slipping between the cracks of existence.

She swallowed hard. "You need to sit down."

He shook his head. "No. If I stop moving now, I won't get back up."

Elara's heart twisted painfully at the quiet acceptance in his tone.

No. She refused to accept that.

Not when she had no answers. Not when she didn't even understand the truth of what had been done to them.

Not when something deep inside her—something instinctive—was screaming that he didn't want to die.

She tightened her grip on him. "Then tell me what to do."

Rowan was quiet for a long moment, his breath uneven. "There's only one way."

Elara braced herself. "What is it?"

His gaze flickered to hers, his expression unreadable.

"You have to let me in."

A sharp chill ran down her spine.

"Let you in?"

Rowan nodded, but his expression was hesitant, almost careful. "The bond—our bond—it's meant to connect us fully. But right now, it's fractured. Unstable."

Her fingers curled against his sleeve. "Because I don't remember you."

His jaw tensed. "Because you don't trust it."

Elara swallowed hard.

A Heartbeat Away From Death

Could she blame herself?

A fae prince had stepped out of her mirror, told her she held his life in her hands, and now expected her to let him in. To accept a bond she couldn't feel, memories she didn't have.

It was madness.

But Rowan—Rowan was dying.

And she couldn't ignore that.

She forced herself to meet his gaze. "What do I have to do?"

A flicker of surprise passed across his face as if he hadn't expected her to agree. But he quickly masked it, his features smoothing into something more composed.

"Close your eyes," he murmured.

Elara hesitated, her pulse thrumming, but she did as he asked.

Darkness.

For a brief moment, it was nothing but the sound of her breathing, the distant howl of the wind outside, the cold press of his fading presence against her skin.

Then—

A heartbeat.

Louder than before.

Not hers. Not his. But something between them.

A pressure settled against her chest, not painful, but heavy. Familiar. Like the moment before waking from a dream, caught between the real and the forgotten.

A rush of something—warm, electric—threaded through her veins. And then—

Images.

Flashes of silver light.

The scent of rain-soaked grass.

A voice, distant but deep, whispering her name with quiet reverence.

Elara's breath hitched.

The memories—

They weren't whole, weren't clear. But they were there. Pieces of a life she had lost—a life bound to him.

And for the first time, she didn't fight it.

She let it happen.

A Heartbeat Away From Death

The bond pulsed.

Her chest ached, but it wasn't painful. It was something else. Something foreign yet familiar, pressing into every space she hadn't known existed.

A connection.

A tether.

And then—

A gasp.

Elara's eyes snapped open just as Rowan collapsed against her, his full weight pressing into her as his body gave out.

She barely caught him, knees buckling beneath its force, but she held on.

And then she heard it.

The second heartbeat.

Strong. Steady.

No longer fading.

Her breath shuddered out of her.

Rowan was still, but he wasn't fading anymore. His body

was solid against hers, his breath warm against her neck. His heartbeat—the one that had always been tethered to hers—was no longer slipping away.

She had saved him.

But as she sat there, heart racing, limbs trembling from the weight of what had just happened, another thought clawed its way to the surface.

This was only the beginning.

And she had no idea what came next.

Six

The Fae and the Mortal Girl

Elara's entire body trembled, but she refused to let go.

Rowan was limp against her, his breathing shallow but steady, his weight pressing into her as she struggled to hold him upright. His golden eyes, so sharp and commanding before, were half-lidded, dulled by exhaustion.

But he was alive.

Barcly.

The second heartbeat inside her, the one that had nearly faded into nothing, was no longer slipping away. It thudded faintly beneath her ribs, still weak and fragile but present. It was tethered to her again, a reminder that his existence depended on her—on a love she wasn't sure she could give.

She swallowed hard, trying to steady her breathing, her mind spinning.

What had just happened?

One moment, she had let him in—let the bond between them flare to life, let something deep and ancient awaken inside her. And now, Rowan was here, slumped against her, alive but barely clinging to this world.

This wasn't fair.

Elara clenched her jaw.

How had she become responsible for something like this?

She had spent her entire life being ordinary. She had gone to school, made friends, and had dreams. And now, suddenly, she was bound to a fae prince by some cruel twist of fate.

This was not her burden.

And yet…

She couldn't ignore how her chest ached at seeing him like this. Weak. Vulnerable. Barely holding on.

"Elara…" Rowan's voice was a whisper, strained and hoarse, but hearing him speak sent a shiver down her spine.

She shifted slightly, trying to support his weight without

sending them both collapsing onto the floor. "I'm here," she said, though she wasn't sure why she said it, why the words mattered.

His fingers twitched, a faint tremor running through them as his grip tightened around the sleeve of her shirt.

"You... feel it, don't you?"

Elara's breath hitched.

The bond.

She did feel it.

Not in a way that made sense—not as love or longing—but as something undeniable. Something raw and ancient, something she could not fight even if she wanted to.

It was there, pulsing between them, threading through her veins like a melody she had once known but forgotten.

And that terrified her.

She pulled away, carefully shifting his weight so that he was leaning against the side of her bed instead of her. Rowan let out a soft groan but didn't resist. He was too weak to protest.

Elara stood quickly, crossing her arms tightly over her chest. "Tell me everything," she demanded, her voice sharper than she intended. "No more riddles. No more half-truths."

Rowan exhaled slowly, his golden eyes flickering open just enough to meet hers. "You already know more than you think."

"That's not an answer."

He was silent for a long moment, then sighed. "The bond between us is... older than you realise."

Elara stiffened. "How old?"

His gaze darkened, and she saw something unreadable in it for the first time.

"Elara," he said carefully, "you've lived this life before."

The words knocked the air from her lungs.

She stared at him, her entire body rigid. "What?"

Rowan's expression was unreadable, but there was something in his gaze—something heavy, something ancient.

"This isn't the first time we've met," he said.

Elara shook her head violently. "No. That's—that's impossible. I would remember."

"Would you?" His voice was quiet. "The curse was designed to strip you of everything. Your memories. Your feelings. Your past."

She took a step back, hands trembling at her sides. "You're lying."

"I'm not."

Her chest rose and fell in uneven breaths, her pulse hammering wildly.

This couldn't be true.

She had lived as a mortal girl in the human world. She had gone to school. She had spent summers at her grandmother's house. She had dreamed of an ordinary future that had nothing to do with fae curses and dying princes.

This was her life.

Wasn't it?

"Elara," Rowan said again, softer this time as if sensing her spiralling thoughts.

She pressed her fingers to her temples, shaking her head. "No. No, this—none of this makes sense."

"I know," he admitted.

Frustration burned through her. "Then explain it to me."

Rowan hesitated but shifted slightly, leaning his head against the bedframe as if summoning the strength to speak.

"The queen—my mother—feared my death. So she did what fae do best." His golden eyes flickered with something dark. "She made a bargain."

Elara swallowed. "With who?"

Rowan's expression hardened. "With fate itself."

A chill ran down her spine.

"She bound my life to another's—to someone who could tether me to this world, keep me from fading." He paused, overseeing her. "She chose you."

Elara let out a bitter, humourless laugh. "Why me?"

Rowan's expression darkened, and for the first time, his gaze flickered with something close to regret.

"Because you were already mine."

The world tilted.

Elara's breath caught, and she forced herself to step back as if putting space between them would somehow undo the weight of his words.

"Stop," she whispered. "Just stop."

Rowan's expression softened. "Elara—"

The Fae and the Mortal Girl

"No." She clenched her fists, anger and confusion twisting together inside her. "You don't get to say things like that. You don't get to make me question my own life."

Rowan exhaled, then leaned forward slightly, bracing his arms against his knees. "You think I wanted this?" His voice was quiet, but there was an edge to it now. "You think I wanted to be bound to someone who would never remember me? Someone who could—" He broke off, jaw clenching, and when he spoke again, his voice was tight. "Someone who could kill me just by choosing not to love me?"

Elara's breath shuddered in her chest.

Because she hadn't thought about it that way.

She had been so caught up in her fear and anger that she hadn't considered what this meant for him.

Rowan wasn't asking for her love.

He was fighting for his life.

The realisation sent a strange ache through her, something more profound than fear, heavier than confusion.

Rowan watched her, his golden eyes steady. "You don't have to believe me," he said finally. "You don't have to trust me. But the truth remains."

He reached out, pressing his palm against the centre of his

chest.

"Our hearts are bound."

Elara's stomach twisted.

Because she could feel it.

The bond.

The weight of it, the way it pressed against her ribs, was like an invisible chain, linking them together in a way that defied logic.

She hated it.

But more than that—she feared it.

Because deep down, in a place she didn't want to acknowledge, she knew.

Rowan was telling the truth.

And whether she wanted to or not—

She was running out of time to decide if she would save him.

Seven

The Queen's Forbidden Spell

The room was drowning in silence.

Elara's heart pounded, but it wasn't just hers. Rowan's heartbeat, which she carried within her, thudded weakly, tethered to her existence by a fragile thread. Their bond pulsed like an ember barely clinging to life, a reminder that every breath he took depended on her.

But that wasn't what unsettled her most.

It was his words.

"Because you were already mine."

She couldn't shake them. I couldn't unhear them.

Her life—her future—her very heartbeat had been stolen from her before she had ever been given a choice.

Elara exhaled sharply, pressing her hands against her temples. "I can't do this right now."

Rowan, still leaning against the bedframe, tilted his head slightly. His golden eyes watched her with an intensity that made her feel exposed, like he saw every frantic thought racing through her mind.

"You have to," he murmured.

She let out a sharp, bitter laugh. "No, I don't. I don't have to do anything." She turned away from him, pacing across the floor. "I didn't ask for this. I didn't ask for a bond, a curse, or to be tied to some fae prince I don't even know."

Rowan didn't argue.

Instead, he said, "Then let me tell you what you should know."

Elara's hands curled into fists. She didn't want to hear it. She didn't want more pieces of a life she had no memory of shoved into her hands like she was supposed to accept them.

But if she walked away now, what then?

Rowan would fade.

And that second heartbeat—the one that had haunted her since childhood—would be gone.

She swallowed the lump in her throat. "Fine," she bit out. "Tell me about the curse. About the bond. About her."

Rowan's expression darkened.

"She is the reason we are bound." His voice was quiet, but there was a cold and distant sharpness. "The Queen of Aendrial. My mother."

Elara stilled.

She had expected this, but hearing it out loud still made her stomach twist.

"What did she do?"

Rowan exhaled slowly. "She made a deal with something ancient. Something that should have never been disturbed."

Elara shivered. "Fae make deals all the time, don't they?"

His jaw tightened. "Not this kind."

The air in the room suddenly seemed heavier, like the space between them had thinned, allowing the weight of something unseen to press down on her skin.

Elara crossed her arms. "Start from the beginning."

Rowan hesitated, then nodded. "My mother was never meant to bear a son," he began. "The Seers predicted she would ruin the realm if she did. They said I was a child of misfortune. That my birth would be a curse upon the face."

Elara frowned. "And yet she still had you."

His golden eyes darkened. "Because she wanted to prove them wrong."

There was something deeply unsettling in the way he said it.

"She thought she could change fate," he continued. "If she was powerful enough, clever enough, she could rewrite the destiny written for me. So when I was born under a dying star when my body began to fade before my first breath—" His throat bobbed. "She did something forbidden."

A chill crept down Elara's spine.

"She stole a heart," Rowan whispered.

The words sat heavy in the air between them.

Elara could barely get the question past her lips. "Whose heart?"

Rowan looked at her then, honestly, and the weight of his gaze made her feel like she was standing at the edge of something too deep, too vast to comprehend.

"Yours."

The Queen's Forbidden Spell

The room blurred.

Elara staggered back, a sharp pulse of panic slamming into her chest.

"No," she choked out. "That's not—That's not possible."

Rowan didn't move. "You were meant to die that night, Elara."

Her vision swam.

"Your fate had already been sealed. But the queen—my mother—tore the threads of fate apart." His voice was steady, but there was something haunted beneath the words. "She ripped your heart from the cycle of mortal life and bound it to mine, forging a link that should never have existed. You survived. But only as half of what you once were."

Elara's breath shuddered. "Half?"

Rowan nodded. "You lived. But you forgot. Because the magic that bound us erased the life you should have had."

She shook her head violently. "No. I—I had a life. I had a family. I—" Her voice cracked. "I'm real."

Rowan's gaze softened, but there was no comfort in it. "You are real," he said quietly. "But you are not whole."

Elara clenched her jaw, forcing back the tears burning at the edges of her vision.

A Curse Between Heartbeats

This wasn't happening.

This was not happening.

She turned away from him, pressing her fingers against her forehead.

But the more she tried to push his words away, the more they tangled into her thoughts, pulling apart everything she had ever believed about herself.

Had she ever really been whole?

Hadn't she always felt like something was missing?

Like a thread of her existence had been cut away before she ever had a chance to grasp it?

Her hands trembled at her sides.

The second heartbeat had never been hers.

Because she had been given to someone else before she even had a chance to live.

"Elara."

Rowan's voice was gentle, but she didn't turn around. She couldn't.

She squeezed her eyes shut. "Why are you telling me this now?"

The Queen's Forbidden Spell

He was quiet for a long moment. Then—

"Because the curse is failing."

Elara inhaled sharply.

Rowan stood, moving toward her, slow and careful. "The queen thought she could manipulate fate, but even she could not control something this unnatural forever. The spell she wove between us is unravelling."

Elara swallowed hard. "And what happens when it does?"

Rowan hesitated. "I fade."

A sharp ache tore through her chest.

He was dying.

The second heartbeat inside her—the one that had never belonged to her—was proof of that.

Rowan exhaled, reaching out to touch her but stopping just before their fingers met.

"Elara." His voice was barely above a whisper. "If the curse breaks completely, your heart may not survive it either."

She went still.

Her gaze snapped to his, wide with fear.

"If I die, you die too."

The words were a blade against her soul.

A terrible, suffocating weight crashed over her.

She had spent her whole life never knowing him, never asking for this connection, never choosing to love him.

But now, if she let him go—

If she let the curse break—

She would go with him.

She was trapped.

Bound to a fate she had never written.

Her heart no longer belonged to her.

And for the first time in her life, she truly felt the weight of it.

Eight

The Shadows That Watch

T he air in the room shifted.

Elara felt it instantly—a ripple of something unseen brushing against the back of her neck, cold and weightless, like the whisper of a ghost. Her skin prickled, her pulse instinctively quickening. The second heartbeat—Rowan's heartbeat—fluttered inside her chest, an unnatural echo of her own.

It was a warning.

She wasn't sure how she knew it, but she did.

Something was watching.

Her fingers curled tightly against her palms as she forced

herself to turn toward Rowan. He stood a few feet away, his golden eyes sharp, his body still weak from their last encounter, but his expression had changed.

He felt it, too.

His gaze flicked toward the window, his jaw clenching.

"Elara," he murmured. "Don't move."

Her breath hitched. "What is it?"

He didn't answer.

Instead, his entire posture tensed, shoulders taut, fingers twitching at his sides like a predator poised to strike.

Then—

A shadow moved outside.

Not the flicker of tree branches against the moonlight, not the simple distortion of light bending through the glass. This was something else. Something wrong.

The darkness outside her window pulsed, shifting unnaturally, watching.

Elara's throat went dry.

Rowan exhaled slowly, his voice just above a whisper. "They

found us."

A cold weight dropped in her stomach.

"They?"

Rowan didn't answer immediately. His gaze remained locked on the shifting shadow outside, the golden light in his irises flickering like a dying flame.

Then, finally—

"The ones who have been waiting for the curse to break."

A chill ran down her spine.

Elara's thoughts spun, searching for an explanation that made sense, but none came.

"What—what do they want?" she whispered.

Rowan's lips pressed into a thin line. "You."

The word sent a bolt of panic straight through her.

She took a step back, her heart hammering against her ribs—both of them. "Why?"

Rowan finally turned to her, his expression unreadable. "Because if they take you, they take me."

A Curse Between Heartbeats

The room felt more minor, the walls pressing inward as her mind reeled.

She shook her head. "No. No, I—I don't understand. Who are they?"

Rowan's gaze darkened. "The Unseen."

A shiver crawled up her spine at the name, as if something inside her recognised it—even though she was sure she had never heard it before.

"The Unseen?" she echoed.

Rowan nodded. "Creatures of the in-between. The watchers of what exists beyond the veil of life and death." His voice was quiet but edged with something grim. "They are drawn to things that should not be."

Elara swallowed hard. "Like us."

Rowan's jaw tightened. "Like the bond."

Her breath came short and fast now, her mind racing.

The curse was unnatural. Rowan had said so himself. A spell that tethered two souls together when one should have died.

And now, something was coming to claim it.

She turned back toward the window, dread curling inside her

stomach. The shadow outside had thickened, stretching taller, bleeding into the edges of the glass like ink in water.

Then—

It moved.

A slow, deliberate shift, like deciding whether to step forward or stay hidden.

"Elara." Rowan's voice was firm now. Urgent. "Listen to me. You cannot let them see you."

She turned sharply toward him. "What?"

"They don't just watch." His expression was grim. "They hunt."

Her stomach clenched.

Panic surged through her veins. "Then what do we do?"

Rowan hesitated for only a moment before making a decision.

"We leave."

Elara blinked. "What?"

Rowan stepped toward her, grabbing her wrist. His touch was still cool but not as fragile as before. He was regaining strength—slowly, but enough to move.

"You can't stay here," he said. "It's not safe anymore."

Elara yanked her arm back. "I can't just leave my life behind!"

Rowan's eyes burned into hers. "You don't have a choice."

She opened her mouth to argue, to demand a better answer, but then—

The room dimmed.

Not like a light being switched off, but as if the darkness outside had seeped into the walls, bleeding into the space around them. The air felt heavier and thicker, making it harder to breathe.

The shadows weren't waiting anymore.

They were coming.

Rowan cursed under his breath. He turned to the nearest reflective surface—Elara's mirror, the shards still broken on the floor—and raised his hand.

A pulse of golden energy flickered at his fingertips, weak but there. He muttered something under his breath, a string of syllables that sent the hair on Elara's arms rising.

The mirror fragments trembled.

And then—

The Shadows That Watch

A tear split through the air.

Not a sound. Not a break.

A tear.

Like the very fabric of the world had been sliced apart.

Elara stumbled back, her stomach twisting at the sight of it—a gash, in reality, itself, a doorway made of light and shadow opening in the space where her mirror once stood.

Rowan turned to her.

"Come with me."

Her heart pounded.

She glanced at the window again, the darkness pressing closer, and the creeping watchers waiting just beyond the glass.

And then she looked at Rowan—at the golden flickers of magic barely holding him together, at the exhaustion in his features, at how he was reaching for her, silently asking her to trust him.

She had no reason to.

No reason to believe him.

I don't think there's a reason to go with him.

A Curse Between Heartbeats

But if she stayed—

The shadows would take her.

The Unseen would claim what they had been waiting for.

And she would never wake up from whatever nightmare this was.

Elara's fingers curled into fists.

Then, before she could let herself hesitate—

She grabbed Rowan's outstretched hand.

The moment their fingers met, the world lurched.

The shadows lunged.

And then—

Everything shattered into light.

Nine

A Prince on the Edge of Oblivion

E lara hit the ground hard.

The impact sent a shock through her bones, knocking the breath from her lungs. The world around her spun, the remnants of golden light fading as she struggled to get her bearings. Cold stone pressed against her palms, smooth and ancient, and when she finally forced her eyes open, she saw... nothing.

Darkness stretched in every direction.

Not the suffocating, heavy kind she had felt when the Unseen had been watching, but an endless, open void—a place that neither belonged to the living nor the dead.

She shivered, slowly pushing herself up. "Rowan?"

A Curse Between Heartbeats

For a moment, there was no answer.

Then, a quiet groan.

Her head snapped toward the sound.

Rowan lay sprawled a few feet away, his chest rising and falling in uneven breaths. His golden eyes were half-lidded, his body weak, his skin unnaturally pale—paler than before.

Something was wrong.

Elara scrambled toward him, ignoring the lingering dizziness in her head. "Rowan!"

He didn't respond.

She reached for him, shaking his shoulder gently, but his body barely reacted. His breathing was shallow; his magic—what little of it she had seen before—was dim.

Panic spiked in her chest.

No.

Not now.

Not after everything.

She pressed her fingers against his wrist, searching for a pulse. There it was—barely. Thready. Weak.

A Prince on the Edge of Oblivion

The second heartbeat inside her, the one that was tied to his, was barely more than a whisper.

Elara's stomach twisted.

This was different from before.

This wasn't just the curse weakening.

This was him fading.

"Rowan, wake up," she demanded, shaking him harder. "You need to wake up."

Nothing.

Elara's breath hitched, fear curling like ice in her veins.

She didn't know what to do.

She didn't know how to help him.

Her fingers curled into the fabric of his shirt, panic creeping closer with every second that passed. "You said I could keep you here. That the bond is what keeps you from fading."

Rowan's lips parted slightly, but no words came out.

Elara clenched her jaw.

Desperation clawed at her throat.

A Curse Between Heartbeats

Think, Elara.

He had told her before—when she had let him in and chosen to accept the bond even for a moment, it had stabilised him and stopped him from slipping further into oblivion.

She had to do it again.

But how?

She took a deep breath, pressing both hands against his chest, right over where his heart should be, where her heartbeat—his heartbeat—was supposed to pulse.

Focus.

She squeezed her eyes shut.

She didn't know what she was doing.

She didn't know if this would even work.

But she had no other choice.

Elara inhaled deeply, centring her thoughts on the bond—on the strange, invisible thread that tied them together, on the heartbeat that had never been hers.

She focused on it.

On him.

A Prince on the Edge of Oblivion

On the life that had been forced into her hands.

A warmth spread from her palms.

A soft, slow pulse—like a flicker of light in the darkness.

Rowan's body jerked slightly, his breath catching in his throat.

Elara didn't stop.

She didn't know what was happening but didn't let go.

The warmth spread further, an invisible thread tightening, weaving, stitching something together.

And then—

A sharp inhale.

Rowan's eyes snapped open.

Golden light flared in his irises, just momentarily, before dimming again. His chest rose sharply, his entire body tensing as if he had been yanked back from the edge of something he wasn't meant to return from.

Elara pulled her hands back, breathing hard.

Rowan gasped for air, his fingers twitching against the stone floor.

"Elara…" His voice was raw, hoarse, but he was awake.

Relief crashed through her so hard she nearly collapsed back onto the ground.

"You idiot," she hissed, her voice shaking. "You were slipping away and didn't even warn me?"

Rowan groaned, rolling onto his side, still catching his breath. "I… didn't think it would happen this fast."

Elara clenched her fists, anger and fear swirling together inside her. "Well, it did."

She wanted to yell at him.

I wanted to demand answers.

But mostly, she just wanted to ensure he wouldn't disappear from her again.

Rowan exhaled, running a hand through his hair before glancing around. "Where are we?"

Elara swallowed hard, looking at their surroundings. "I was hoping you could tell me."

The endless stretch of nothingness surrounded them, and yet… there was something about it that felt ancient.

Rowan's gaze darkened. "The In-Between."

Elara frowned. "The what?"

"It's the space between worlds," he said, voice quiet. "Between life and death. Between the fae realm and yours."

A shudder crawled down her spine. "Why are we here?"

Rowan's expression was grim. "Because I was dying."

The words sent a sharp pang through her.

Dying.

It was getting worse.

Faster than either of them had realised.

Elara clenched her jaw. "Then we need to fix this. We need to figure out how to break the curse before—"

Before he disappeared for good.

Rowan gave a hollow chuckle. "Breaking it won't be easy."

Elara exhaled sharply, standing to her feet. "I don't care if it's not easy, Rowan. We don't have a choice anymore."

Rowan looked up at her, something unreadable in his expression. Then, slowly, he nodded.

"You're right."

Elara blinked.

He wasn't arguing.

That was new.

Rowan pushed himself up, though he still looked unsteady. "There's only one place we can go if we want to find answers."

Elara narrowed her eyes. "And where's that?"

He met her gaze.

"The Forgotten Archives."

A strange chill ran through her at the name.

Something about it felt... familiar.

Rowan noticed how her breath caught and hesitated, and his golden eyes flickered with something knowing.

"You've been there before," he murmured.

Elara swallowed hard.

More memories she didn't have.

More pieces of a life were stolen from her.

She straightened her shoulders. "Then take me back."

Rowan studied her for a moment. Then, finally, he nodded.

"This way."

He turned, stepping toward the unseen path ahead.

Elara hesitated only for a moment.

Then, she followed.

Ten

A Heart Split in Two

Elara followed Rowan through the endless, shifting void of the In-Between, her heart thundering in her chest. Or was it his? The second heartbeat—the one that tethered her to him—was stronger now than before, but it still felt wrong. Fragile. Unstable.

Rowan's steps were slow, deliberate, his golden eyes scanning the space around them. She wanted to ask if he knew where he was going, but something about how he moved—like he was fighting against an unseen current—kept her silent.

They had almost lost him.

Again.

Elara clenched her fists, the memory of his near-disappearance still too raw in her mind. The way he had collapsed, his pulse weakening, slipping toward nothingness. She had felt it happen inside her, the fading heartbeat, the unraveling bond.

She had saved him.

But for how long?

"How much time do we have?" she asked, her voice barely above a whisper.

Rowan didn't look at her. "I don't know."

Elara exhaled sharply, frustration curling inside her. "That's not an answer."

His gaze flicked toward her then, unreadable. "It's the only one I have."

The weight of his words pressed against her ribs.

He wasn't just guessing.

He knew his time was slipping through his fingers like sand in an hourglass, and he didn't know when the last grain would fall.

She hated it.

Elara turned away, her eyes scanning the path ahead—if it could even be called that. The In-Between wasn't a place, not in the way the human world was, or even the fae realm. It was nothingness stretching infinitely in all directions.

Yet somehow, Rowan knew where to go.

Or at least, she hoped he did.

"How do we get to the Forgotten Archives?" she asked.

Rowan exhaled, as if steadying himself. "The same way we got here."

Elara frowned. "Which is…?"

His lips pressed into a thin line. "Through the bond."

A sharp pulse ran through her, like a plucked string deep inside her chest. She stopped walking. "What does that mean?"

Rowan turned to face her fully. "The bond between us isn't just a curse," he said carefully. "It's a path."

Elara stared at him. "A path to what?"

"To what was lost," Rowan murmured. "To the memories buried beneath the spell."

A strange pressure tightened in her chest. "You mean—"

"Yes," Rowan said before she could finish. "The Forgotten Archives hold the truth about the curse. About what the queen did. About us."

Elara's stomach twisted.

The idea of remembering—of unlocking whatever had been stolen from her—was terrifying.

Because what if she did remember?

What if everything Rowan had said was true?

What if she had loved him before?

What if she had chosen this fate once and had it ripped away?

Elara took a shaky breath. "And what happens if I can't open the path?"

Rowan hesitated. "Then I fade. Permanently."

A cold, sharp silence settled between them.

Elara's fingers curled at her sides.

She was trapped.

The Unseen hunted them. The curse was unraveling. The bond was unstable. And now, she was the only one who could open the way forward.

She lifted her gaze to Rowan's. "Tell me how."

He hesitated, his golden eyes searching hers. "You're certain?"

"No," she admitted. "But I don't have a choice."

Rowan nodded slowly. "Then close your eyes."

Elara swallowed hard, then obeyed.

Darkness surrounded her.

Not like the In-Between—this was deeper, heavier, something curling around her ribs like unseen hands.

She inhaled sharply, feeling the second heartbeat in her chest.

It was steady now.

Stronger.

She reached for it, focusing, letting the bond between them pulse like a thread stretching into the unknown.

A whisper of something—faint, distant—brushed against her mind.

A memory.

A voice.

"Don't forget me."

A Heart Split in Two

Elara gasped, her eyes snapping open.

The world shifted.

For a split second, she was elsewhere.

Not in the In-Between. Not in the human world. Not in the fae realm.

Somewhere else entirely.

The air was thick with magic, swirling in silken ribbons of silver and blue. A towering structure stood before her—tall, endless, made of stone that shimmered as if it were alive. The Forgotten Archives.

She had found it.

Rowan exhaled sharply beside her. "You did it."

Elara barely heard him. Her mind was still reeling, the whisper echoing inside her skull.

"Don't forget me."

It had been her voice.

She clenched her fists, forcing herself to focus. She could fall apart later.

Right now, they had work to do.

"Let's go," she murmured.

Together, they stepped forward.

The air shifted again as they crossed into the Forgotten Archives.

Elara barely had time to process it before a sharp pang ripped through her chest.

She staggered, gasping.

The second heartbeat—Rowan's heartbeat—thudded erratically.

Something was wrong.

Rowan caught her by the arm. "Elara?"

She clutched her chest, struggling to breathe. "I—I don't know."

The pain twisted deeper.

Then—

A vision slammed into her.

A storm of memories.

Flashes of a life she had never known—yet somehow had lived.

A Heart Split in Two

A silver lake beneath a starless sky.

Fingers entwined with hers.

A whispered promise: "No matter what happens, I will find you."

Elara gasped as the vision shattered, her knees buckling.

Rowan caught her before she hit the ground.

"Elara!" His voice was sharp, but it sounded far away.

She could barely breathe.

Because she knew now.

She remembered.

Her heart wasn't just his—

It had always been his.

The curse hadn't stolen her life.

It had stolen her choice.

And now, she had to decide—

Would she fight it?

Or would she let fate take him away again?

Eleven

A Name I Once Knew

The Forgotten Archives loomed around Elara, vast and endless, a labyrinth of stone and shadow. The walls pulsed with a faint, eerie glow, casting flickering silver light against towering shelves filled with ancient tomes, scrolls, and artifacts that seemed to hum with power. The air was thick with something unseen, something that pressed against her skin like the whisper of a forgotten memory.

But none of that mattered.

Because Elara was still on her knees, gasping for breath, her mind unraveling at the edges.

She had seen something.

Felt something.

A name—just on the tip of her tongue. A name she once knew, a name that wasn't hers, yet belonged to her all the same.

Rowan crouched beside her, his golden eyes sharp with concern. "Elara. Look at me."

She couldn't.

Not yet.

Her chest ached, her heartbeat thundering wildly—both of them. Her own, rapid and panicked. Rowan's, still uneven, still fading, but steady enough to remind her that he was here. That she hadn't lost him—not yet.

But she had lost him before.

Hadn't she?

The vision had been too real. The silver lake. The voice whispering against her skin.

"No matter what happens, I will find you."

She squeezed her eyes shut, pressing her palms against the cold stone beneath her.

A past she didn't remember was clawing its way into the present.

And it hurt.

A Name I Once Knew

"Elara," Rowan tried again, his voice softer this time, careful. "Tell me what you saw."

She swallowed hard, forcing her breath to steady. She lifted her gaze to his, and the moment their eyes met, another wave of recognition slammed into her.

She had looked into those eyes before.

She had loved those eyes before.

She shook her head, gripping the edge of her sleeve. "I—I don't know."

Rowan's expression darkened. "You do know."

She wanted to deny it. Wanted to tell him that she was still the same girl she had always been, that she wasn't hiding pieces of herself inside a past life she had no memory of.

But she couldn't lie.

Not to him.

Not when something deep inside her was screaming for her to remember.

Elara exhaled shakily. "I saw…" Her voice wavered. "A lake. Silver water. No stars."

Rowan stilled.

His fingers clenched against the stone floor. "And?"

Elara hesitated. "A promise."

The weight of the word settled between them, thick and heavy, a thread pulling at the bond that tethered them together.

Rowan's breath came slow and steady, but there was something behind his eyes now—something raw. "What kind of promise?"

Elara's throat tightened.

She hadn't just seen a promise.

She had felt it.

She pressed a hand against her chest, against the bond that tied her heartbeat to his. "It was real, wasn't it?" she whispered. "We... We knew each other before this."

Rowan didn't speak.

Didn't confirm it.

Didn't deny it.

But he didn't have to.

The silence was answer enough.

Elara closed her eyes for a brief second, her mind racing. "What

A Name I Once Knew

was my name?"

Rowan sucked in a quiet breath.

She looked at him again, pleading now. "If I really knew you—if I really chose this bond—then tell me. Who was I?"

His jaw tightened.

For a moment, she thought he wouldn't answer.

But then—

A whisper.

Barely a breath.

A name.

"Aeris."

The world shuddered.

Elara's body went rigid, something ancient and unfamiliar pulling at her, twisting in her gut like a thread being unraveled too fast.

Aeris.

The name crashed against her like a wave breaking against the shore.

Not hers. Not Elara's.

But she knew it.

It felt like a lost melody, something buried so deep in her soul that it had become part of the silence.

She let out a shuddering breath.

Rowan was still watching her, his golden eyes careful, waiting. "Do you remember?"

Elara swallowed hard. "I don't know."

She wanted to.

She needed to.

But the memories weren't hers to claim yet. They hovered just out of reach, like whispers through fog, slipping through her fingers before she could hold onto them.

Still, the name left a mark, pressing against the fragile pieces of her mind, demanding to be known.

Aeris.

She let the name settle against her tongue.

A past self.

A Name I Once Knew

A life that had been erased.

And Rowan—

Rowan had known her.

She met his gaze again, this time with something sharper, something desperate. "Tell me everything."

Rowan exhaled, his expression tightening. "I don't know how much time we have—"

"I don't care."

Rowan hesitated.

Then, finally, he nodded.

"You weren't just anyone," he murmured. "You were—"

A sound cut him off.

A deep, slow creaking.

Like something ancient awakening.

Elara's breath hitched. She turned toward the towering shelves surrounding them, her heart pounding. The Forgotten Archives had been silent since they arrived. But now—

Now something was moving.

Rowan pushed himself to his feet, his body still unsteady. "We're not alone."

Elara swallowed, forcing herself to stand. "Who else would be here?"

Rowan's gaze flickered toward the shifting shadows between the shelves. "Not who," he said grimly.

The silver light pulsing from the walls dimmed, flickering like a candle in the wind.

And then—

A whisper.

Not inside her head this time.

Not part of the bond.

A real voice, slithering through the stillness of the Archives.

"You should not have come."

Elara froze.

The shadows between the shelves thickened, curling like tendrils, spilling forward like something alive.

Rowan moved before she could react, stepping in front of her. "Stay behind me."

A Name I Once Knew

Elara opened her mouth to argue—

But then the shadows took shape.

A figure emerged from the darkness, shifting and flickering as if it was barely holding its form. It had no face, no eyes, just an endless void of blackness that pulsed with the same eerie energy that had chased them through the human world.

One of the Unseen.

Elara's stomach dropped.

The creature tilted its head slightly, its voice like ice scraping against stone.

"The Forgotten Archives do not belong to you."

Rowan tensed. "We need answers."

"And yet," the creature murmured, its form pulsing, "you have found only more questions."

Elara's blood turned to ice.

Because it was right.

She had come here for truth.

But all she had found was another piece of a puzzle she didn't know how to solve.

The name.

Aeris.

Hers, yet not hers.

The past was clawing its way back.

But so were the shadows.

And they were running out of time.

Twelve

The Other Half of the Curse

The Unseen loomed before them, a shifting shadow wrapped in darkness. It had no eyes, no discernible face, but somehow, Elara felt its gaze—felt it in her bones, in the cold weight pressing against her chest.

The Forgotten Archives, once eerily silent, now hummed with unseen energy. The walls pulsed with dying light, as though the presence of the Unseen had tainted the very air.

Rowan stood rigid, his golden eyes locked onto the creature. His magic, though weak, flickered at his fingertips—a faint glow of embers in the dark.

"You should not have come," the Unseen whispered again. Its voice was like a thousand echoes layered over one another, crawling under Elara's skin.

Rowan clenched his jaw. "We came for answers."

"And you will not find them here."

Elara's breath hitched as the creature's form twisted unnaturally, its tendrils of darkness curling between the towering shelves of ancient tomes.

Her fingers curled into fists. "We don't have time for riddles. If you know something about the curse, tell us."

For a long moment, there was silence.

Then—

A low, grating sound.

Laughter.

A shiver ran through her.

"You misunderstand, child." The Unseen's voice turned cold, unfeeling. "You do not need to find the other half of the curse. It will find you."

Elara's pulse slammed against her ribs. "What does that mean?"

The creature didn't answer.

Instead, the darkness around it began to shift.

Rowan moved fast, grabbing Elara's wrist and yanking her back. "Move!"

The moment her feet left the ground, the shadows lunged.

A force like icy fingers wrapped around her, clawing at her skin, dragging at the bond inside her chest. She choked on a gasp as something pulled, something unnatural, as if trying to rip her apart.

Rowan snarled, golden light sparking from his fingertips. He sliced through the tendrils of darkness, forcing them back with a burst of magic.

The Unseen hissed.

Elara stumbled, her legs trembling, but she forced herself to stay upright.

Rowan turned to her, his face pale but determined. "We have to go. Now."

She barely had time to nod before he grabbed her hand again and pulled her deeper into the Archives.

The towering shelves stretched endlessly before them, the stone beneath their feet shifting as if the very ground was alive. The deeper they ran, the more the shadows twisted, curling like vines, reaching for them.

Elara's chest burned.

A Curse Between Heartbeats

The second heartbeat inside her pounded hard, erratic and wild, as if responding to something unseen.

Something waiting.

Then—

A flash of silver light.

A whisper, deep in her mind.

You were never meant to be whole.

Elara staggered, a sharp pain lancing through her skull. The vision came suddenly, violently—

A throne room bathed in moonlight.

A woman with silver eyes, draped in shadow, her fingers dripping with power.

Rowan—on his knees, blood on his hands.

And her—standing beside him, her heart no longer her own.

Then—

Pain.

A fracture.

The Other Half of the Curse

A curse.

Elara gasped, her knees nearly buckling. Rowan caught her before she hit the ground.

"Elara!"

She blinked rapidly, her breath coming in quick, shallow bursts. "I—I saw something."

Rowan's expression darkened. "What did you see?"

Elara swallowed hard. "The other half of the curse."

A long silence stretched between them.

Then—

A slow, careful whisper.

"Yes."

Both she and Rowan snapped their heads toward the voice.

A figure stood at the end of the passage between the bookshelves. Unlike the Unseen, this one had a shape—a tall, slender figure cloaked in shadows. Its presence was suffocating, an unnatural cold creeping into the air.

Elara's fingers dug into Rowan's arm.

The figure took a step forward.

"You have always been only half of what you were meant to be."

Rowan tensed beside her. "Who are you?"

The figure tilted its head.

"I am the memory that was stolen. The truth that was buried."

Elara's heart stopped.

A memory.

Buried.

A lost part of her.

The figure's voice softened, curling around her mind like silk.

"You wish to break the curse, child? You cannot, unless you know what was taken from you."

Elara's throat tightened. "What do you mean?"

The figure extended its hand.

"Let me show you."

Rowan moved before she could react, stepping between them, his golden eyes ablaze. "You're not touching her."

The Other Half of the Curse

The figure let out a sound—something between a sigh and a chuckle.

"And yet, she has already been touched by fate, Prince Rowan. You cannot stop what has already begun."

Elara felt it before she saw it.

A ripple of energy, deep inside her.

Her name—the one Rowan had spoken—

Aeris.

The air shattered around her.

Her vision ripped open.

And then—

She remembered.

She remembered everything.

The silver lake.

The night Rowan had knelt before her, promising to never let her go.

The Queen's spell, the way her heart had been severed, her soul split in two—one half given to Rowan to save his life. The other locked away, lost to time.

Her love.

Her choice.

Her life.

Everything stolen.

Everything broken.

Elara's breath hitched. Her body trembled as reality crashed down on her.

Rowan was saying something, but she couldn't hear him.

She was trapped in the weight of it all.

Because she had made this choice.

Once.

Long ago.

And now, she had to make it again.

The figure's voice curled around her mind one last time.

"The curse was never meant to be broken, child. Only completed."

The Other Half of the Curse

The air stilled.

Elara's eyes snapped open.

Rowan reached for her, his golden eyes burning with fear.

And then—

The shadows consumed her.

Thirteen

The Court of the Unseen

The darkness swallowed Elara whole.

It was not like closing her eyes. It was not like stepping into a shadowed room. It was deeper than that—more final, more wrong. It was the kind of darkness that felt. It pressed against her skin like unseen hands, whispering against her ears in a language she did not understand.

She wasn't falling.

She wasn't moving at all.

She was simply taken.

Her breath came fast and uneven, but there was no air, no space, no world around her. Only them.

The Court of the Unseen

The Unseen.

She could feel them now.

Not just one or two, but many.

They hovered in the abyss, shifting through the darkness like flickering shadows at the edge of perception. Not bound by flesh or form, not bound by time or place—just watching.

Always watching.

A heartbeat pulsed faintly in her chest.

Not hers.

Rowan's.

The bond was still there—thin, stretched, distant—but still there.

A sharp, breathless panic gripped her. Where is he?

She had seen his golden eyes, his hand reaching for her—then nothing.

She tried to move, but there was no ground beneath her, no gravity to pull against. She was trapped in the emptiness, an invisible thread tethering her to something unseen.

And then, a voice.

"You have come before us, child of two worlds."

It was not one voice.

It was many, layered over one another, ancient and hungry.

Elara's body tensed. "Where am I?"

"You stand in the Court of the Unseen."

A weight pressed down on her at those words, crushing and invisible, curling around her soul rather than her body.

The Court of the Unseen.

A place whispered about in fae stories, in the forgotten pages of history.

A place where time did not exist.

Where those who had been erased still remained.

Elara swallowed hard. "Why am I here?"

A ripple of movement surrounded her.

Then—

Light.

Not sunlight, not flame.

The Court of the Unseen

A pale, eerie glow flickered in the distance, illuminating the figures that had been nothing more than shadows before.

They were not human.

And they were not fae.

Elara's breath caught in her throat.

The Unseen had no faces, no true forms—only outlines of what they used to be. Some appeared tall and skeletal, others fluid and shifting like mist. Their eyes—if they could be called eyes—were hollow voids, endless pits of silver and black.

One stepped forward.

It moved without moving, its form shifting, twisting.

"You carry what was stolen. A bond that was never meant to be."

Elara clenched her jaw. "The curse."

A sound rippled through the space around her—a low, distorted hum, neither laughter nor speech.

"A curse, a gift, a punishment.'"

The voices wove together, speaking as one yet separate, like echoes from different directions.

Another figure stepped closer, its form unraveling at the edges.

"Do you know what you are, child?"

Elara forced herself to stand taller. "I know that I was stolen. That my heart was never mine."

Silence.

Then—

"And yet you do not understand."

A sudden, sharp pain lanced through her chest.

She gasped, gripping her ribs, feeling the bond inside her pulse like an open wound.

Images flashed through her mind—Rowan kneeling in the silver lake, a whispered name, a tear in the fabric of fate itself.

The Unseen had seen it all.

They had watched her die.

They had watched her be reborn into a life that was never meant to exist.

Elara clenched her teeth. "Tell me, then."

The figures loomed closer.

The Court of the Unseen

"You were not just stolen, child. You were divided."

The air cracked around her.

The pain in her chest deepened.

Elara struggled to breathe. "What—what do you mean?"

The tallest of the Unseen tilted its hollow head.

"You were never meant to be one."

Something inside her snapped.

A flood of memories tore through her, unbidden and violent—

—A girl in a darkened throne room, her hands bound in golden chains.

A voice whispering words of power, of separation.

A blade, gleaming silver.

Two bodies lying on the cold stone floor.

One soul.

Torn in half.

Elara's knees buckled.

"No," she gasped. "No, that's not—"

But she knew.

She had felt it all along.

The emptiness inside her. The sense of something missing, something she could never name.

She wasn't just cursed.

She was split.

One part of her had been given to Rowan, tethered to him, keeping him alive.

But the other half—

Her breath hitched.

"Where is it?" she whispered.

A terrible stillness filled the Court.

Then, the whisper of truth.

"Lost."

Elara's blood ran cold.

"What do you mean, lost?" she demanded. "It has to be

somewhere—"

The Unseen's voices wove together, threading through the very air.

"It is nowhere. It is everywhere."

She shook her head, panic creeping into her voice. "No. That doesn't make sense."

The Unseen shifted, the space around them warping.

"Your soul is incomplete, child. The bond with the prince was only half the spell. The other half was cast into the void, scattered across time itself."

The weight of it settled deep inside her, crushing.

A piece of her was missing.

Not just stolen.

Shattered.

Rowan hadn't just been cursed.

She had.

She had spent her life searching for something she didn't know was gone.

The ache in her chest, the loneliness, the whispers in the back of her mind—it had all been leading her here.

Elara's hands trembled.

"How do I get it back?"

The Unseen laughed.

A sound of impossibility.

"You do not."

A cold terror clawed through her ribs.

"No." Her voice wavered. "There has to be a way—"

The Unseen's whispers curled around her like a noose.

"You are only half a soul, child. You cannot be whole. Not unless you undo what has been done."

Her breath came fast and ragged. "Undo?"

A long silence stretched between them.

Then—

A whisper.

A warning.

The Court of the Unseen

"To reclaim what is lost, you must sever what remains."

The bond.

Rowan.

Elara's stomach dropped.

She barely heard the crack of reality splitting behind her—

Barely felt the golden light pulling her away—

Before she was ripped from the Court of the Unseen.

Fourteen

The Betrayal in His Eyes

Elara's breath ripped from her lungs as she was pulled back through the void, the Unseen's whispers still curling around her like invisible threads, clinging to her skin, to her soul.

She didn't remember falling.

She only remembered the truth.

She had been split in half.

The bond tethering her to Rowan was not the curse in its entirety. It was only one half of a broken spell, a magic so unnatural it had fractured the very essence of who she was.

Her soul had been divided.

The Betrayal in His Eyes

And the Unseen had confirmed her worst fear—her missing half was gone, scattered into the fabric of existence itself.

Unless...

Unless she undid what had been done.

A violent pull yanked her from the abyss, and suddenly, the weightless nothingness shattered into reality.

Elara hit the ground hard, the force of the impact knocking the air from her chest. Her vision blurred with pain, stars bursting behind her eyes. The cold press of stone scraped against her palms as she gasped for breath.

She was back.

Back in the Forgotten Archives.

A dim silver glow flickered from the towering shelves of books, and the faint hum of magic still pulsed through the air.

But something was wrong.

The bond inside her ached.

No longer distant. No longer stretched thin by the abyss.

It was close.

Strong.

Rowan.

She felt him before she saw him.

His presence thrummed through the space between them, tethered to her like an invisible thread woven into her very existence.

Elara pushed herself up, still dizzy, still raw from the truth she had been given.

And then—

She saw him.

Standing at the far end of the Archive chamber.

Watching her.

His golden eyes burned like wildfire beneath the dim light, unreadable, dangerous.

But something was different.

Something in his posture.

Something in the way his fingers curled at his sides, as if holding back an unseen force.

"Elara." His voice was quiet, but there was an edge to it. A tension she had never heard before.

The Betrayal in His Eyes

A chill crawled up her spine.

She had seen fear in Rowan before.

She had seen desperation.

But this…

This was something else.

Something cold.

Elara's breath came fast. "Rowan, I—"

He took a step forward.

She flinched.

The air between them pulsed tight, the bond inside her twisting sharply.

"You were taken," he said, his voice too calm. "By the Unseen."

Elara swallowed hard. "Yes."

His golden eyes flickered. "And they told you something."

She hesitated.

A heartbeat passed.

A Curse Between Heartbeats

The second heartbeat inside her thundered.

Rowan's expression hardened.

"They told you about the other half of the curse."

A sharp pang twisted inside her chest.

Elara's mouth went dry.

He already knew.

She could see it in the way he stood, the way his breath came slow and measured, as if bracing himself for what came next.

A sick feeling curled in her stomach.

"How long?" she whispered.

Rowan's jaw tensed.

She took a step closer. "How long have you known?"

His silence was answer enough.

Elara's breath caught.

She stumbled back a step, her pulse pounding. "You knew. This entire time, you—"

"Elara." Rowan's voice was tight, like something was unraveling inside him.

But she didn't care.

"You knew," she repeated, her voice shaking. "You knew that my soul was broken. That I've been missing something my entire life. And you—"

Her chest ached, fury and betrayal tangling together like wildfire in her veins.

"You didn't tell me."

Rowan's lips parted, but no words came out.

Because what excuse could he give?

There wasn't one.

Elara clenched her fists. "How could you keep this from me?"

Rowan exhaled, his breath uneven. "Because you didn't need to know."

The words cut her deeper than she expected.

She let out a bitter laugh, shaking her head. "I didn't need to know?"

Rowan took another step toward her. "Elara, listen to me—"

"No," she snapped.

His golden eyes darkened.

"Elara, you don't understand what's at stake—"

She laughed again, but it was empty, hollow.

"No, Rowan. I think I understand perfectly."

She swallowed hard, the weight of it settling in her chest.

"My entire life," she whispered, "I have felt like something was missing. Like a part of me was just… gone. And now, I finally know why."

Rowan's lips pressed into a thin line.

She stepped forward now, voice shaking. "And the worst part? You knew. You knew, and you still let me believe I was whole."

A muscle twitched in his jaw. "I did it to protect you."

Elara's blood boiled.

"You don't get to decide that for me," she hissed.

His golden eyes flashed. "I didn't have a choice."

Elara laughed sharply. "There's always a choice, Rowan. And you chose to lie to me."

Silence crashed between them.

The bond inside her pulled, pulsed, twisted.

Rowan clenched his fists. "You don't understand, Elara."

Her vision blurred with rage.

"No," she whispered, voice breaking. "I think I finally do."

And then—

The second heartbeat inside her stuttered.

Rowan flinched, a flicker of something raw passing over his face.

A realization slammed into her.

The bond.

It was reacting to her.

To her anger.

To her pain.

To her doubt.

Rowan's eyes widened. "Elara—"

But it was too late.

The bond weakened.

A sharp, searing pain tore through her chest.

Rowan stumbled, his breath catching.

"No," he gasped, golden light flickering around him like dying embers.

Elara's pulse raced.

The bond was breaking.

Not completely.

Not yet.

But it was fracturing.

A warning.

Rowan swayed on his feet, breathing hard. "Elara, stop—"

But she couldn't stop.

Because something inside her had already been broken.

Long before she ever met him.

The Betrayal in His Eyes

Long before this curse.

A part of her had always been missing.

And now, for the first time—

She knew it was his fault.

She met his gaze, and for the first time, she saw it—

The betrayal in his eyes.

Fifteen

Love Is Not a Chain

The air between them was heavy, thick with unspoken words and raw, unfiltered anger.

Elara's heart—Rowan's heart—pounded inside her chest, an uneven rhythm that mirrored the chaos twisting inside her. The second heartbeat had always been there, a quiet, constant presence that had haunted her for as long as she could remember.

Now, it felt like a shackle.

A chain he had forged.

Rowan was still standing across from her, shoulders tense, golden eyes burning with something she couldn't name. Desperation? Guilt?

Love Is Not a Chain

It didn't matter.

Because she couldn't trust him anymore.

Elara clenched her fists, ignoring the sharp pain lancing through her ribs as the bond—the curse—wavered between them. "How long?" she demanded.

Rowan's breath came shallow. "Elara—"

"How long did you plan to keep me in the dark?" Her voice was sharp, shaking with fury. "Would you have ever told me? Or were you just going to keep lying until you faded away?"

His jaw tightened. "I wasn't lying."

Her laugh was bitter, hollow. "Oh, really? What do you call hiding the truth from me, then?"

Rowan exhaled sharply, his hands curling into fists at his sides. "I did it to protect you."

She hated those words.

Another chain, another excuse.

"Protect me from what?" she snapped. "My own life? My own past?"

His golden eyes darkened. "From making a choice you can't undo."

A sharp chill ran down her spine.

A choice.

To sever the bond.

To undo the curse.

To let him go.

Elara's throat tightened.

Her anger wavered—not gone, but shifting, twisting into something heavier.

Because she could feel it now.

She could feel how weak he was.

How much the bond was fraying, how the thread between them was unraveling at the edges.

And how much he was afraid.

Not for himself.

For her.

Elara swallowed hard. "If I break the bond, I die too."

Rowan didn't answer right away.

Love Is Not a Chain

And that silence—that hesitation—

It told her everything.

Elara's breath hitched. "You knew that too."

Rowan's golden eyes flashed with something raw, something aching. "Yes."

Her body locked up.

Her stomach dropped.

She wanted to scream, to rage at him, but the words caught in her throat, choking her.

Because this wasn't just about the curse anymore.

This was about him.

About how he had never planned to survive this.

He had never meant to burden her with a choice.

Because he had always intended to fade away first.

"Unacceptable," she whispered.

Rowan's brows furrowed. "Elara—"

"You were just going to let yourself die?" Her voice cracked.

"Were you ever going to tell me before you disappeared forever? Or were you just hoping I wouldn't notice?"

Rowan took a step forward, his eyes blazing. "Of course I was going to tell you—"

"When?" she demanded, her voice sharp as a blade. "When it was too late? When I had no choice left at all?"

His breath came uneven, his fingers trembling.

Elara could see it—

The weight he carried.

The fear.

Not of dying.

Of her knowing the truth.

Rowan exhaled sharply. "I would have rather let myself fade than force you to bear the weight of this curse."

Her vision blurred.

The betrayal—

The anger—

It was still there, burning in her chest, searing through her veins like wildfire.

But beneath it—

Beneath it was something worse.

A terrible, sinking grief.

Because despite everything, despite his choices, despite the lie of omission—

Rowan had never chained her to him out of selfishness.

He had been trying to set her free.

And she didn't know if that made it better—

Or so much worse.

She turned away from him, pressing her fingers to her temples, trying to breathe through the storm inside her.

"I don't know what to do," she admitted, her voice barely above a whisper.

Rowan was quiet for a long moment.

Then—

"I don't either."

That confession was what finally broke her.

Because it was the first time he had ever admitted it—

That he wasn't in control.

That he wasn't the powerful fae prince who had all the answers.

That he was just as lost as she was.

Elara let out a shaky breath. "Love isn't supposed to be a chain, Rowan."

His expression flickered with something haunted.

"I know."

Elara's fingers curled against her sleeves. "But that's what this is, isn't it?"

Rowan hesitated. Then, slowly, he nodded.

"A bond that was never supposed to exist."

A bond that kept him alive.

A bond that kept her trapped.

Elara clenched her jaw.

A choice.

Love Is Not a Chain

That's what this came down to.

She had one choice—

Stay bound to him, stay tethered, stay chained—and keep both of them alive in this fractured existence.

Or—

Break the bond.

Shatter the curse.

Sever what was left of her soul.

And take both of them down with it.

She let out a shaky breath. "I don't want you to die."

Rowan flinched. "Elara—"

"I don't," she repeated, sharper this time. "But I also don't want to be a prisoner in this bond forever."

A long silence stretched between them.

Then Rowan's voice—soft, quiet, resigned.

"Neither do I."

Elara's pulse stuttered.

A Curse Between Heartbeats

She met his gaze—

And for the first time, she saw it.

Acceptance.

Not of his fate—

But of hers.

Of the fact that this was her choice to make.

Not his.

Not fate's.

Hers.

A sharp pang twisted inside her, her body trembling with the weight of it.

Because no matter what she chose—

Someone would break.

Either him.

Or her.

Or maybe—

Maybe both.

Elara exhaled slowly, grounding herself in the moment, in the weight of Rowan's gaze, in the bond that still pulsed faintly inside her.

"I need time," she whispered.

Rowan nodded. "Then take it."

Another beat of silence.

Then—

"For now, we find another way," he murmured.

Elara swallowed hard, nodding. "For now."

But they both knew—

Time was already running out.

Sixteen

The Fade Begins

The first thing Elara noticed was the cold.

It wasn't the kind of chill that settled on the skin, the kind that came with wind and winter. No—this was deeper. Sharper. It curled around her bones, sank into her chest, seeped into the space between her ribs like an invisible weight.

She shivered, rubbing her arms, trying to shake it off.

It didn't work.

Rowan sat across from her, silent, staring at nothing. His golden eyes—once burning, once alive—had dimmed. The light behind them flickered like a candle struggling against an unseen wind.

The Fade Begins

Something was wrong.

Something had changed.

She swallowed hard. "Rowan?"

His gaze snapped to her. For a moment, she thought she saw something familiar in his eyes—concern, recognition.

Then, nothing.

His expression smoothed over, his body unnaturally still.

A chill crawled down her spine.

Elara shifted closer. "Are you okay?"

He didn't answer.

Instead, his fingers twitched at his sides, like they were forgetting how to hold their shape.

Then—

A flicker.

A thin wisp of golden light unraveled from his fingertips, curling into the air like smoke. It vanished before it touched the ground.

Elara's breath hitched.

No.

No, this wasn't happening.

She reached for him, fingers brushing against his wrist—cold.

Not just his usual fae-cool temperature.

Ice.

Her pulse thundered. "Rowan."

Still, he said nothing.

Then—

Another flicker.

This time from his shoulder, a faint golden mist slipping from his skin, dispersing into the air.

Fading.

Elara's chest tightened.

She grabbed his arm, shaking him harder than before. "Rowan, look at me."

His head turned, slower than it should have. His eyes met hers, but they were hazy, distant.

The Fade Begins

Like he was already half gone.

Panic clawed its way up her throat. "No. No, you are not doing this right now."

Rowan exhaled shakily, a weak smirk tugging at his lips. "I don't think… I have a choice."

The sound of his voice—ragged, thin, wrong—made something inside her splinter.

She felt it now.

The bond.

It was weakening.

Not just fraying at the edges like before—splitting.

A steady unraveling, thread by thread, pulling Rowan further and further away from her.

Her breathing came faster. "What do I do? How do I stop this?"

Rowan let out a slow breath. "You can't."

Elara refused to accept that.

"There's always a way." She squeezed his arm, trying to ground him, trying to pull him back into her reality, her presence. "You just need to hold on."

A flicker of amusement crossed his face. "I am trying."

More golden mist slipped from his skin.

His fingers trembled, his form flickering like something that wasn't quite real anymore.

She felt the bond inside her strain, pulling apart at the seams.

Elara clenched her jaw. "Why is this happening?"

Rowan's voice was softer now. "The bond is breaking faster than we thought."

Her stomach dropped.

"How?"

He didn't answer.

Because they both knew.

Because of her.

Because of the doubt, the anger, the betrayal still lingering in her chest.

The bond was tied to her emotions—to her choices.

And she had pulled away.

The Fade Begins

Even if she hadn't meant to.

Even if she hadn't realized it at the time.

Elara felt something deep inside her crack.

Rowan was slipping through her fingers.

She couldn't let this happen.

She squeezed his hand, fingers tight against his cooling skin. "Rowan. Stay here. With me."

His breath came uneven now. "Trying..."

His golden eyes dimmed further.

The flickers of magic curling from his skin grew more frequent, his body shimmering at the edges like something half-forgotten.

Elara panicked.

"No, no, no, you don't get to fade away now!" She leaned closer, gripping his shoulders. "I am not going to let you die!"

A soft chuckle. "You might not... have a choice."

Her vision blurred.

She shook her head, ignoring the way her hands trembled

against him.

There had to be a way to fix this.

There had to be a way to stop it.

"Elara."

His voice was so weak now.

She barely heard him over the frantic pounding of her heartbeat—his heartbeat.

She forced herself to look at him, really look at him.

His expression was softer now, almost peaceful.

Like he had already accepted this.

Like he wasn't afraid anymore.

A sharp, unbearable ache bloomed in her chest.

Because she was afraid.

Terrified.

Elara shook her head, her hands gripping him tighter, as if holding on harder could stop the inevitable. "No. You don't get to leave me again."

The Fade Begins

Rowan's lips parted slightly. "Again?"

Her breath caught.

A flicker of something—something buried deep—shuddered through her mind.

A memory.

A flash of silver light.

A night filled with whispered promises.

A goodbye she had once given.

A choice she had once made.

Elara's body went rigid.

Rowan saw the look in her eyes, the shift in her expression, and something in him changed too.

"Elara."

This time, he said it like a prayer.

Like he already knew.

Like he was remembering too.

The bond inside her ached, pulsed sharply.

She gasped, gripping her chest as pain flared through her ribs.

Rowan let out a shaky breath, his body flickering again, his magic thinning.

Elara squeezed his hands, tears burning behind her eyes.

She was losing him.

But now, she remembered.

She had lost him before.

And she had vowed—promised—to never let it happen again.

Her breath came ragged.

A choice.

That's what this came down to.

And for the first time—

She knew what to do.

She knew how to stop him from fading.

Elara let out a slow, steadying breath.

Then she met his gaze, her hands still gripping his.

The Fade Begins

And she let go.

Not of him.

Not of the bond.

But of the anger.

The resentment.

The doubt.

She let herself remember.

The life before.

The love that had once been real.

The choice she had made to save him—not because of a curse, not because of fate, but because he was hers.

Because she had chosen him once.

And she chose him again now.

The bond flared.

A burst of golden light erupted between them.

Rowan gasped, his body jerking as the magic rushed back into him, pulling him back from the edge of oblivion.

The flickering mist stopped.

His hands—his form—solidified again.

Elara gasped for air, her body shaking as the magic settled.

Rowan's breath came hard and fast.

His golden eyes—bright again, alive again—locked onto hers.

"Elara…"

She exhaled sharply. "I'm here."

A long silence stretched between them.

Then Rowan reached for her, his fingers curling over hers.

And this time—

She didn't pull away.

Seventeen

A Love That Never Belonged to Me

Elara's fingers trembled as she held onto Rowan's hand, his skin still too cold, his form still too fragile, as if the magic keeping him tethered to existence was barely holding on.

The bond inside her pulsed, stabilizing, but she felt the weight of something much deeper pressing against her ribs—an aching truth she could no longer ignore.

This love—this bond—had never belonged to her.

It had been forced upon her.

Stolen.

Twisted into something unnatural, something that had rewritten who she was before she ever had the chance to choose.

And now, standing in the dim glow of the Forgotten Archives, with Rowan's golden eyes searching hers for something she couldn't give, Elara felt the full weight of that betrayal crash over her.

Her breath hitched, her chest tightening as the memories stirred—fragments of a past life she couldn't fully grasp, a love that had once been hers but had been torn away, fractured into pieces she had no hope of reclaiming.

Rowan must have felt the shift in her, because his grip loosened ever so slightly. "Elara," he murmured.

She flinched.

Not at the sound of his voice—she had always found comfort in that, even before she knew why.

But at the way he said it.

Like he already knew.

Like he could feel the truth unraveling inside her.

"Elara," he said again, softer this time, as if gentleness could change what she had come to realize.

This wasn't her love.

A Love That Never Belonged to Me

Not anymore.

She had been someone else once. A girl named Aeris, a girl who had loved a fae prince so much that she had given her very soul to save him.

But Elara wasn't Aeris.

And that love—that devotion—that choice—had never belonged to her.

Her stomach twisted painfully, the weight of it nearly suffocating.

She tore her gaze away from Rowan, staring at the ancient shelves of the Archives, at the dust-covered tomes that held secrets no one was ever meant to uncover.

This place had been built on forgotten things.

Lost memories.

Shattered pasts.

She understood now why she had been drawn here.

Because she was one of those forgotten things, wasn't she?

A shadow of a girl who had once made an impossible choice.

Rowan shifted closer. "Tell me what's wrong."

She almost laughed at that.

Almost.

Because everything was wrong.

She wanted to scream at him, to demand why he had let her believe she could be whole when she was missing a part of herself.

Why he had let her think this love was real when it had been forced upon her, when the bond had been forged in desperation, not in choice.

She wanted to tell him it wasn't fair.

That she deserved better than this.

That she deserved a love that hadn't been woven into a curse.

But Rowan was looking at her like he already knew all of that.

Like he had always known.

Elara clenched her fists, breathing through the storm raging inside her. "This love," she whispered, her voice hoarse, "it isn't mine."

Rowan inhaled sharply, his fingers twitching against hers.

"Elara—"

She shook her head, stepping back. "No. Don't. Don't tell me it is. Because it's not."

Rowan's jaw tightened, his golden eyes flickering with something close to pain.

"Elara, you were Aeris."

The words sent a shiver down her spine.

She had been Aeris.

Once.

A lifetime ago.

But she wasn't anymore.

That girl—that version of her—was gone.

All that remained was the shattered pieces of what she had been, a fractured soul bound to a man who was barely clinging to existence.

"I'm not her," Elara whispered.

Rowan didn't speak.

Didn't argue.

Because he knew.

He had always known.

His love belonged to someone who no longer existed.

Elara exhaled shakily, pressing a hand against her chest, against the heartbeat that didn't belong to her, the heartbeat that had never belonged to her.

She had spent her whole life feeling like something was missing.

And now she knew why.

Because she wasn't whole.

Because she had never been whole.

"Elara," Rowan murmured, and for the first time since she had met him, he sounded truly afraid.

Because he knew what came next.

She did too.

She lifted her gaze to his, meeting his eyes for what might be the last time.

"I can't be who you need me to be."

Rowan flinched.

She had thought he would fight her on it. Thought he would

try to tell her she was wrong, that she was still Aeris, that she was still the girl who had loved him enough to save him.

But he didn't.

He just stared at her.

Silent.

Still.

Because he knew.

And accepting it hurt more than fighting it ever could.

The bond inside her shuddered, an echo of something once unbreakable now beginning to unravel.

Rowan swallowed hard. "If you sever the bond—"

"I know," Elara cut in. "If I sever the bond, we both die."

A long, tense silence stretched between them.

Then Rowan exhaled, slow and steady.

His expression softened—not in surrender, not in defeat, but in understanding.

He wasn't going to stop her.

He wasn't going to beg her to stay.

Because he knew—

Love was not a chain.

It wasn't something that could be forced, something that could be stolen from a past life and forced upon the present.

Elara blinked hard against the burning in her eyes. "I want to choose."

Rowan nodded once. "Then choose."

She inhaled, shaky, unsteady.

Then she let go.

Not of the bond.

Not yet.

But of the weight she had been carrying.

She wasn't Aeris.

She wasn't a girl who had once given up her soul for love.

She was Elara.

And her love—her choices—would be hers alone.

Even if it meant breaking everything.

Even if it meant losing him.

A single tear slipped down her cheek.

Rowan watched her, silent, waiting.

Waiting for her to decide if this love could still be saved.

If she wanted to save it.

If she could.

Elara closed her eyes.

And she chose.

Eighteen

The Final Beat

The world had never been so silent.

Elara stood frozen, the weight of her decision pressing down on her ribs like an iron cage, trapping her in a moment that felt stretched thin—fragile, like it might shatter beneath the force of her next breath.

Across from her, Rowan didn't move.

He just stood there, watching her with those eyes—golden, endless, burning with something between sorrow and acceptance.

The bond between them throbbed, the last, trembling thread of magic that held them together fraying, unraveling at the edges like fabric worn too thin.

The Final Beat

Rowan had said nothing.

He hadn't begged her to stay.

Hadn't tried to change her mind.

Because he already knew.

She could feel that he knew.

This was the end.

The final beat.

The moment where everything unraveled.

Elara's breath came slow, shaky. She pressed her hand over her chest, where two heartbeats pulsed—one hers, one his, entangled together in a magic older than she could comprehend.

A magic that was breaking.

A magic that she was about to shatter completely.

She swallowed hard, her fingers curling against the fabric of her sleeve. "Rowan," she whispered.

His jaw tensed slightly, as if bracing for impact.

But his voice was steady. "Say it."

A Curse Between Heartbeats

Elara's throat tightened.

Her chest ached.

Because the truth—the decision she had made—was going to hurt both of them.

And yet—

She wasn't Aeris.

She had never been herself because of this bond.

Because of this curse.

And if she wanted to be free—if she wanted to be real—

She had to let him go.

Her fingers trembled as she reached for him one last time, brushing against his wrist, his skin cool beneath her touch.

Rowan inhaled softly, his eyes never leaving hers.

Elara's voice broke. "I can't live like this."

A flicker of pain flashed across his face.

But he nodded.

Because he understood.

The Final Beat

Because he had always understood.

A tear slipped down Elara's cheek, and she felt the bond pulse weakly in response. Rowan's heartbeat—inside her—shuddered like a dying star, barely holding on, waiting for her to sever it completely.

"I'm sorry," she whispered.

Rowan closed his eyes.

Then—

She let go.

And everything collapsed.

The bond snapped.

A violent, shattering force ripped through her, a sensation so sharp, so sudden, it felt like she was being torn apart from the inside out.

Her body jerked, her knees buckling as something deep within her cracked open, releasing a pulse of raw magic into the air.

And Rowan—

Rowan let out a sharp, ragged gasp, his entire form flickering as the golden light that had always surrounded him dimmed, shuddering, failing.

"No—" Elara lunged for him, her fingers curling into his shirt, but it was too late.

The magic binding him to this world had been the bond.

And she had just severed it.

Rowan swayed, his breath uneven, his entire body unraveling before her eyes.

Elara's vision blurred with tears. "No, no, I—"

Her chest ached, her hands gripping him tightly, refusing to let go even as she felt the warmth of his magic dissipating, his presence slipping like sand through her fingers.

Rowan stared at her, his golden eyes softening, his lips parting as if to speak—

But no words came.

Only a faint, broken exhale.

His fingers brushed against hers one last time.

And then—

Rowan faded.

A swirl of golden light, dissolving into the air.

The Final Beat

Gone.

Elara screamed.

Her body collapsed forward, hitting the ground hard, her fingers clawing at the empty space where he had just been.

Nothing.

There was nothing left.

No warmth.

No second heartbeat.

No Rowan.

A raw, fractured sob tore from her throat, her chest heaving, her entire body shaking as she pressed her palm over her ribs—

Where his heartbeat had once been.

Now, there was only one.

Hers.

Alone.

Elara gasped for air, her vision swimming as the weight of what she had done crushed her, dragging her down, drowning her in the silence that followed.

The world felt different now.

Lighter.

Colder.

As if something essential had been stripped away.

As if part of her had just died with him.

She had broken the curse.

She had freed herself.

And in doing so—

She had lost him forever.

A hollow ache settled deep in her bones, an emptiness she couldn't even begin to understand.

Because she had thought—

Even for a moment—

That when she let go…

Maybe he would still exist.

Maybe there would be a way to fix it.

The Final Beat

But Rowan was gone.

There was no undoing this.

No second chance.

No more golden eyes looking at her like she was his entire world.

Just silence.

Just her.

Alone.

Elara closed her eyes, pressing her forehead against the cold stone floor, her body wracked with silent sobs.

She had made her choice.

And now, she had to live with it.

But she didn't know how.

Because the final beat had fallen.

And there was no one left to hear it.

Nineteen

A Curse Undone, A Soul Unraveled

The silence was unbearable.

Elara lay on the cold stone floor, her body curled inward as though she could physically hold herself together—as though she could stop the unraveling before it consumed her entirely.

But she couldn't.

Because Rowan was gone.

The second heartbeat—his heartbeat—had vanished, leaving only a hollow ache in her chest, a deep, unbearable void where something precious had once been.

The curse was undone.

A Curse Undone, A Soul Unraveled

And she had done it.

Her choice.

Her will.

The magic that had once bound them together had shattered at her command, leaving nothing behind but emptiness.

And yet—

The pain did not leave with it.

If anything, it had grown, stretching through her veins, settling in the marrow of her bones like an echo of the bond that was no longer there.

Elara gasped for air, her lungs straining, her pulse thundering in her ears—the only heartbeat left in her body.

She had thought that once she was free, she would feel whole.

But now—

Now she felt fractured in a way she couldn't explain.

A curse undone.

A soul unraveled.

She forced herself to sit up, though the motion sent sharp pangs of pain through her ribs, like something inside her was still fighting against what she had done.

Her fingers curled against the cold floor of the Forgotten Archives, pressing into the dust-covered stone as if she could ground herself in this reality.

But it was a reality without him.

A life without the tether of Rowan's presence.

She had thought she would feel free.

Instead, she felt like a ghost.

Like she had been severed from something she couldn't live without.

Her breath shuddered out of her. "Rowan…"

His name was a whisper.

A plea.

A wound.

But the air did not answer.

The world did not shift.

There was no flicker of golden light.

A Curse Undone, A Soul Unraveled

No warmth curling at the edge of her vision.

No second heartbeat stirring inside her chest.

He was truly gone.

Elara clenched her teeth, willing herself to stand despite the trembling in her limbs.

She needed to leave.

She couldn't stay here, trapped in the place where everything had ended.

Where she had undone the one thing that had been keeping Rowan alive.

She turned, forcing her legs to move, ignoring the sharp pull of exhaustion in her limbs.

The Forgotten Archives stretched before her, vast and endless, its towering shelves of ancient tomes still pulsing with a dim, fading light.

But something felt different.

The magic here—once suffocating, thick with centuries of forgotten history—was weakening.

Like the moment Rowan disappeared, something else had begun to crumble.

Elara pressed a hand against the nearest shelf. The stone was still solid beneath her fingers, but the magic within it—

It was dying.

The Archives had always existed in the space between realms, a place untouched by time, a refuge for forgotten knowledge and stolen memories.

But now, the threads holding it together were fraying.

Elara's stomach twisted.

Had the curse been tied to more than just her and Rowan?

Had breaking it shattered something far bigger than she had realized?

She swallowed hard, pushing forward.

She had to get out.

She needed answers.

She needed—

A sharp pulse of magic stopped her mid-step.

Elara's entire body tensed, her breath catching as the air shifted around her.

A Curse Undone, A Soul Unraveled

Something was coming.

A ripple of energy, deep and ancient, curled through the room, sending a shiver down her spine.

She turned sharply, scanning the shadows between the bookshelves, her heart hammering.

She had broken the curse.

But what had she woken in its place?

The dim glow of the Archive's magic flickered once, twice—then died completely.

Elara's breath hitched.

Darkness swept in, thick and absolute.

For a terrifying moment, she saw nothing.

Just void.

Just emptiness.

Then—

A whisper.

Soft.

Unfamiliar.

"You were never meant to walk this path alone."

Elara's blood turned to ice.

She spun toward the voice, but there was no one there.

Just shadows stretching between the ancient shelves, just the faint echo of something unnatural stirring in the air.

Her pulse pounded.

"Who's there?" she demanded, her voice sharper than she felt.

Silence.

Then, a low, melancholy hum.

A sound that sent a wave of recognition crashing over her.

Elara's breath caught in her throat.

Because she knew that sound.

She had heard it before.

In the whispers of the Unseen.

In the depths of her unraveling memories.

A Curse Undone, A Soul Unraveled

In the space between dreams and reality.

It was the echo of something lost.

A piece of her that had been taken.

A soul that had been divided.

Her stomach clenched.

Because the curse had been undone.

And yet—

The void had not released its hold on her.

It was still watching.

Still waiting.

Still hungry.

She felt it now, curling at the edges of her mind, whispering in a language she almost understood—

A warning.

A truth.

She had severed the bond.

But she had not severed herself.

The part of her that had been lost—the half of her soul that had been cast into the void when the queen's spell was first cast—

It was calling to her.

It had always been calling to her.

And now that the bond with Rowan had been broken—

Now that there was nothing left tethering her to him—

The void was ready to claim her instead.

Elara's breath hitched.

Her hands shook.

She had undone the curse.

She had unraveled the spell.

But in doing so—

She had opened the door to something worse.

And now, it was coming for her.

Her lips parted, her heart slamming against her ribs in a single, desperate beat.

The final beat.

The one that told her—

This wasn't over.

Not even close.

Twenty

A Soul Unraveled

Elara stumbled back, her breath ragged as the darkness surrounded her. The Forgotten Archives were dying; with it, something else was unravelling—something deep inside her, something she had barely begun to understand.

The void was **calling to her**.

Not just whispering, not just watching.

It was **reaching**.

And it was **hungry**.

She could **feel it now**, curling around the edges of her mind, threading through her skin like an unseen force that had always been waiting, **waiting for her to be alone**.

She had severed Rowan.

She had undone the curse.

And now—

The price had come **due**.

Her heart **slammed** against her ribs as the darkness **rippled**, twisting around the stone shelves of the Forgotten Archives. The very walls **quivered** as though reality itself was folding inward.

Elara clenched her fists, grounding herself against the pull of the void. "I broke the curse," she whispered. "I should be free."

The air **shuddered** at her words.

Then—

A voice.

Soft. Cold. **Ancient**.

"Did you think fate would let you go so easily?"

Elara's pulse **stuttered**.

The voice did not come from the shadows.

It came from **inside her**.

A sharp, burning **pulse** flared in her chest—where Rowan's heartbeat had once been.

She gasped, clutching at her ribs as the pain **spread**, seeping through her bones and sinking into her veins like liquid ice.

It was wrong.

It was **so wrong**.

Rowan was **gone**.

But the **bond**—

It was **not empty**.

Something **else** had taken its place.

Elara fell to her knees, her breath coming in **shallow bursts**, her vision **blurring** as a force she could not see **wrapped around her**.

"You severed the bond."

The voice was **closer now**, like fingers dragging through her mind.

"You thought it would end with him."

A sharp, **jagged laugh** echoed in her skull.

"But you were never just his, were you?"

Her breath hitched.

No.

No, this wasn't—

"The Queen never bound you to him alone."

Elara **froze**.

Her fingers dug into the cold stone floor, her stomach **twisting** as the words **sank into her**.

"The other half of the curse," she whispered.

Not just Rowan.

Not just a love stolen from another life.

Her **soul**.

The part of her that had been **ripped away**.

The part of her that had been **lost to the void**.

And now—

Now, it had come back for her.

Elara gritted her teeth, forcing herself to her feet. Her knees wobbled beneath her, her entire body **screaming** from the weight of the unseen force pressing down on her.

"I won't let you take me."

The air **rippled**, shifting in response to her defiance.

"You think you have a choice?"

The darkness **lunged**.

Elara **threw herself back**, barely dodging the tendrils of shadow that coiled toward her like grasping hands. The moment they **missed**, the air trembled again—

And the **pain inside her chest doubled**.

She **cried out**, collapsing against one of the towering bookshelves as the force inside her **pulled tighter**.

"You were never whole."

The voice **hissed** inside her mind, threading through her thoughts, weaving into the very fabric of her being.

"You cannot live without what was taken."

Elara gasped for breath, her vision swimming. "Then give it back," she rasped.

Silence.

Then—

The world **shifted**.

The void **pulled inward**, collapsing around her like a storm. The magic in the Forgotten Archives—**fading, unravelling**—**rushed toward her**, wrapping around her body in tendrils of silver mist.

And then—

A sharp, violent **snap**.

Elara's **mind cracked open**.

Memories **rushed in**.

Not of Rowan.

Not of the past life she had once lived.

But of something **else**.

Something **deeper**.

Something that had been **stolen the night the curse was cast**.

A room filled with moonlight and smoke.

A **queen's trembling hands** glowing with unnatural magic.

A voice, soft and broken—her voice.

"Don't do this."

"You were never meant to be one."

A scream.

A **shattered soul**.

A Curse Between Heartbeats

A life torn apart and **scattered into the void**.

Elara **gasped** as the vision shattered around her. She clutched her chest, her body trembling, her mind **spinning** from the weight of what she had just seen.

Not just a **bond with Rowan**.

Not just **a stolen love**.

She had been **divided**.

And part of her had been **given away**.

"Who took it?" she whispered, her voice **shaking**.

The shadows coiled, shifting like a living thing.

Then—

A whisper, soft as death.

"The one who created the curse."

Elara **froze**.

The **queen**.

Rowan's mother.

She had not simply **bound Elara to Rowan**.

She had taken **half of her very soul** and **sealed it away**.

Elara's hands **trembled**.

Her heart **pounded**, raw and uneven, as the final, terrible **truth** crashed over her.

She had never been free.

Not from the moment she had been **born into this life**.

Her choices, her thoughts, her **very existence**—

They had never been **hers alone**.

The void shuddered, rippling around her like a predator **waiting to devour its prey**.

"You have a choice now, child."

The words curled around her, dark and **twisting**.

"Stay as you are—broken, fading, incomplete."

The tendrils of darkness slithered closer.

"Or reclaim what was stolen."
Elara's breath came **shallow**, her pulse hammering.
A choice.
A price.
A **soul unravelled**.
And the **only way out** was to take back what had been lost—
Even if it cost her everything.
She lifted her gaze to the void.
"I want it back."
The shadows **smiled**.
And then—
The world **collapsed into darkness**.

www.ingramcontent.com/pod-product-compliance
Lightning Source LLC
LaVergne TN
LVHW021238080526
838199LV00088B/4570